EDUCATING C
WITH AUTISM SI

Educating College Students with Autism Spectrum Disorders is one of the first books to specifically address the accommodation of students with significant learning differences in postsecondary education. Developed with the support of Autism Speaks, and piloted at Pace University, each component of this book is scientifically based and provides a model of emerging best practices for college instruction involving students with ASD. The text is designed to give college faculty a deep understanding of students with ASD and help faculty to productively engage students with ASD, while also meeting the needs of all students in their classes. The strategies included in the manual are solidly grounded in principles of universal design and will prove indispensable for teaching college students of varying ability levels and diverse learning styles.

Dianne Zager is Michael C. Koffler Professor in Autism and Director of the Autism Specialist Advanced Certification Program at Pace University, where she founded and directed the Center for Teaching and Research in Autism and the OASIS College Support Program. She was founding co-editor of the journal *Focus on Autism and Other Developmental Disabilities.*

Carol Alpern is Director of the Communication Sciences and Disorders Program at Pace University. She is a licensed speech-language pathologist, and has the Certificate of Clinical Competence and Specialty Board Recognition in Child Language from the American Speech-Language and Hearing Association.

Barbara McKeon is Director of Aaron Academy, a private special education program serving students in grades 6 to 12, as well as a licensed speech-language pathologist. She holds an Advanced Certificate in Autism from the University of Vermont and has studied Critical Issues in Urban Special Education Institutes at Harvard. She is currently on the faculty at Pace University and is enrolled in a doctoral program at Seton Hall University.

Susan Maxam is University Director for Student Success at Pace University. She is currently enrolled in a doctoral program in Higher Education Leadership and Social Justice at Union Institute & University.

Janet Mulvey is an assistant professor and an educational supervisor in a college support program at Pace University. She received her PhD from Fordham University, and has also served as a school principal and teacher.

EDUCATING COLLEGE STUDENTS WITH AUTISM SPECTRUM DISORDERS

DIANNE ZAGER
CAROL ALPERN
BARBARA MCKEON
SUSAN MAXAM
JANET MULVEY

Routledge
Taylor & Francis Group

NEW YORK AND LONDON

Please find the companion videos on www.autismspeaks.org

First published 2013
by Routledge
711 Third Avenue, New York, NY 10017

Simultaneously published in the UK
by Routledge
2 Park Square, Milton Park, Abingdon, Oxon OX14 4RN

Routledge is an imprint of the Taylor & Francis Group, an informa business

Library of Congress Cataloging-in-Publication Data
Berkell Zager, Dianne, 1948–
  Educating college students with autism spectrum disorders /
  Dianne Zager, Carol Alpern, Barbara McKeon, Susan Maxam,
  Janet Mulvey.
      pages cm
    Includes bibliographical references and index.
  1. Autistic people–Education (Higher)–United
  States–Handbooks, manuals, etc. 2. Autism spectrum
  disorders–United States–Handbooks, manuals, etc. I. Title.
  LC4813.B47 2012
  371.9'0474–dc23   2012008624

ISBN: 978–0–415–52437–7 (hbk)
ISBN: 978–0–415–52438–4 (pbk)
ISBN: 978–0–203–11110–9 (ebk)

Typeset in Minion
by Keystroke, Station Road, Codsall, Wolverhampton

CONTENTS

PREFACE   vii

1   **The New Inclusion Frontier**   1
    A Free and Appropriate Education for All   2
    Prevalence of Students with ASD in Postsecondary
        Education   3
    Autism Spectrum Disorders   6
    The Role of Colleges and Universities   16
    Summary   19

2   **In the Classroom**   21
    Faculty Perceptions of Students with ASD   21
    Learning Needs and Challenges of Students with ASD   24
    Strategies for Effective Teaching   36
    Summary   50

3   **Case Studies**   53

4   **Annotated Resources**   59
    Autism   59
    Universal Design for Learning and Disability-Friendly
        Environments   71

School-based Professional Development Resources
   for Faculty 84
Comorbidity and Autism (Anxiety and Depression) 87
Self-determination 89

APPENDIX A 98

APPENDIX B 105

REFERENCES 109

INDEX 115

PREFACE

The strategies in this text are based on the tenet that all students have the right to an inclusive education among their same-age peers to the maximum extent possible. Through accommodating the instructional needs of students with autism spectrum disorder (ASD) in college courses, providing out-of-class academic coaching, helping students self-advocate, and utilizing ancillary supports as needed, faculty can enable young adults with ASD to succeed in college and go on to lead productive lives as adults. In all cases where a student has gained entrance to a college or university, it is the institution's responsibility to do all it can to enable that student a fair chance at success.

Educating College Students with Autism Spectrum Disorders has been written with support from Autism Speaks. This book is intended for use as a manual by college faculty. The text provides an understanding of students with autism spectrum disorders and is intended to help faculty productively engage these students while continuing to meet the needs of all students in their classes. The strategies included are grounded in the principles of the Universal Design for Learning (UDL) and are evidence-based best practices for instruction. They should prove useful for teaching college students of varying abilities with diverse learning styles, and hopefully will foster enhanced college outcomes for people with autism and related disorders.

The central theme of the manual is that Universal Design for Learning is good for everyone, and that access to learning can be enhanced by broadening our own minds and thinking creatively as we meet the needs of different students. For too long, educators have been trying to meet only the needs of typical learners in their classes. We need to expand our concept of education by moving away from old-fashioned thinking about how to reach a particular type of learner as we begin to think about how to include all learners, including those with learning challenges that can be significant, such as autism.

Methods presented in the manual were developed from a comprehensive review of extant literature and have been piloted in a college support program for students with ASD. Each individual component of the model presented is scientifically based. The package of strategies is put forth as a model of emerging best practices for college instruction. Further research on the newly configured model is underway, as it is believed that the combined power of these practices is significantly greater than that of the individual strategies used in isolation.

In preparation for the manual, two surveys were conducted – one survey was designed to identify faculty needs for working with students with ASD, and the other to learn about concerns and needs of students who are on the spectrum. Professors were asked to describe specific issues they had encountered with students with learning differences in their classes and how they had addressed these issues. Students were asked about their previous education successes and struggles, and their concerns about college. They described perceived areas of difficulty in college classes, along with comments regarding types of instruction and supports that have helped them in their studies. Information gleaned from the surveys has been incorporated into the manual.

The manual has four sections. **Chapter 1** explains the legal mandates regarding students' educational rights and college/professorial responsibilities, and why students with ASD are arriving in greater numbers at colleges. It then describes the main characteristics of autism and some common accommodations for these students. **Chapter 2** is a strategy section that considers specific learning characteristics and styles of students with ASD, and provides recommended approaches and techniques for engaging and assessing students on the spectrum. To further illuminate how to incorporate these strategies into the academic setting, case studies are presented in **Chapter 3**. These examples highlight student and faculty experiences, and illustrate approaches that have proven successful in dealing with challenging situations. Finally, **Chapter 4** provides an extensive list of annotated resources for learning more about teaching and supporting students on the autism spectrum.

Royalties from the Routledge publication of the manual will be donated to Autism Speaks in appreciation of the Autism Speaks funding that enabled us to create the manual and accompanying video. We hope that the publication of this manual promotes quality education for students with autism through the information presented and resultant royalties.

Appreciation is extended to MetSchools for the creation and support of the Michael C. Koffler Professorship in Autism at Pace University and to Autism Speaks for its support of this project.

Dianne Zager

1

THE NEW INCLUSION FRONTIER

This introductory section provides a brief historical overview of legislation regarding students' educational rights and college/professorial responsibilities, explains why students on the autism spectrum are arriving in greater numbers at colleges, then discusses salient characteristics of young adults on the autism spectrum, before describing some common accommodations that colleges can provide. It sets the stage for the major sections of this manual, which are intended to help college faculty understand and engage students with autism spectrum disorder (ASD) in their classes. Through information presented in Chapters 2 and 3, strategies will be explained in relation to specific student learning characteristics. The ultimate goal of the manual is to demonstrate how to facilitate academic learning and enhance success for college students with ASD.

A Free and Appropriate Education for All

The composition of classrooms in U.S. schools has changed since 1975 when the Education for All Act (Public Law 94-142) was passed, a groundbreaking law in education and civil rights. Since 1975, children with special needs have had the right to a free and appropriate education in the least restrictive (i.e., most inclusive) setting. The concept of a free and appropriate education is referred to by special educators as FAPE. The mandate of FAPE that children be educated in the least restrictive school setting possible resulted in children with disabilities receiving their education among nondisabled peers in general education classes (i.e., inclusion). The inclusion movement has been a slow process, but one that has continued; thanks to the commitment of parent advocacy groups, legislators, professional organizations and educators. Despite bumps in the road, political friction, and occasional setbacks, PL 94-142 has been reaffirmed several times over the past four decades, culminating in the Individuals with Disabilities Education Act (IDEA) in 2004.

It has taken many years for the impact of IDEA to reach postsecondary education. Finally, students that have benefitted from the educational rights movement have come up through the school system and today are seeking a college education. Increasing numbers of students with learning differences, including autism, have been educated in inclusive high schools among their peers. By receiving appropriate supports beginning in early childhood and extending through secondary school, students have been enabled to succeed. As students with ASD have mastered rigorous academic subject matter, and have shown themselves to be intelligent, they have debunked myths of intellectual incompetence. Now they want to continue their education among their friends, who are moving on to college. These young men and women have earned the right to a college education, and colleges need to catch up and join the national momentum to include all learners. We need to get ready to do a better job educating students with learning differences. We college professors need to understand the characteristics and learning needs of students with learning differences, and we must accommodate these students without diluting the integrity of our course requirements. College has become the new frontier to continue the hard won inclusion that is now in place at the elementary, middle, and secondary levels (Grigal & Hart, 2010).

In 2009, the U.S. Department of Education brought together stakeholders and experts to examine issues related to post-secondary education for students with intellectual disabilities and developmental disabilities, including autism. The National Institute on Disability and Rehabilitation Research, Office for Postsecondary Education, and Office for Special Education Programs came together for the first State of the Science Conference on Postsecondary Education (U.S. Department of Education, 2009). The meeting brought together participants from various branches of the government and colleges/universities to discuss next steps to improve and increase access to quality postsecondary education for students with disabilities. By providing much needed information to college faculty, this manual is directed toward meeting the critical need for improved postsecondary education, as explicitly expressed at the meeting on the State of the Science Conference on Postsecondary Education.

Prevalence of Students with ASD in Postsecondary Education

Increased numbers of youths with ASD have been educated in inclusive kindergarten through 12th grade classes; however, too often they remain in secondary schools after their peers without disabilities have graduated. Because many students with disabilities continue in secondary school through 21 years of age, the age discrepancy broadens between them and students without disabilities in their schools; so that students who grew up being educated in inclusive classes find themselves no longer in age-appropriate inclusive situations. This situation has led to the need for alternative education environments.

Historically, youth with ASD have not had the opportunity to attend college. However, nearly four decades of free and appropriate public education under the Individuals with Disabilities Education Act have raised expectations and created a need for institutions of higher education to provide educational opportunities for individuals with significant disabilities (Barbour, 2008). Barriers to the provision of inclusive post-secondary education have been (a) low expectations and inadequate preparation (Stodden, Yamamoto, & Folk, 2010), (b) lack of available supports and services in institutions of higher education (Camarena & Sarigiani, 2009), (c) negative attitudes in academic cultures (Clark, 2010), (d) lack of faculty knowledge to accommodate diverse learners (Yell, Ryan, Rozalski, & Katsiyannis, 2009), and (e) lack of access to financial support (Jesien, 2009). There exists a dire need for programs to enable people with ASD to live among their peers, perform activities of their choice in their communities, and expand society's capacity to provide opportunities for all its citizens.

Between 1994 and 2006, the number of children 6 to 17 years old identified with ASD in public schools increased from 22,684 to 211,610, approximately 90%. According to a study conducted by Kogan et al. (2009), it is estimated that 673,000 people in the USA have autism spectrum disorders. Kogan and his colleagues cite figures from the Center for Disease Control indicating that 1 in 90 children between the ages 3 and 17 are on the autism spectrum. With the increasing numbers of children and youth on the spectrum, widespread inclusion of students with disabilities in public secondary schools, and more young adults with disabilities ready for college, the demand for improved transition services and postsecondary support has grown dramatically.

Colleges must provide accommodations to ensure equal education opportunities and to prepare all students for productive adult lives (Boyle, 2000; Dwyre, Grigal, & Fialka, 2010; Eisenman & Mancini, 2010). The movement to improve postsecondary education options is supported in the literature (Briel & Getzel, 2005; Briel & Wehman, 2005; Magliore, Butterworth, & Hart, 2009), showing that postsecondary education experiences lead to better employment and adult living outcomes for individuals with disabilities.

The magnitude of the problem is evidenced by statistics in national and state level reports on employment and adult living outcomes. For example, the 2009 Annual Performance Report of the New York State Education Department shows that the total number of students aged 15–21 receiving special education services in the state during 2007–08 was 56,553. Of these thousands and thousands of students, a devastatingly low rate of positive transitions to employment was reported, most especially for students in the big cities (New York State Annual Performance Report, 2009). While this report highlights the need for improved college support services in New York, the state's low employment rate for individuals with autism is mirrored across the nation.

Legislative Initiatives: A National Perspective

The President's New Freedom Commission on Mental Health (Executive Order 13263, 2002) and Developmental Disabilities Assistance and Bill of Rights Act of 2000 address weaknesses in services to prepare people with disabilities for productive adult lives. The Americans with Disabilities Act of 1990 provides a framework to address the need for supports to fully include all people in their communities. The New Freedom Initiative (2001) recognizes that people with disabilities need a complete and appropriate education to join their communities as equal members.

The 1978 amendments to the Rehabilitation Act of 1973 recognize the problems of low employment and insufficient integration of people with disabilities in their communities. The Act calls for models to promote inclusion and to foster full participation. In order to meet the purposes of the Act, educators will need to enable students who, heretofore, have not participated in college environments to engage fully in academic, social, and career development opportunities.

Colleges are at the forefront of career preparation and productive community involvement. There is a rising call to action for colleges and universities to provide services and supports for the large number of students with learning differences waiting to gain access to an appropriate college education. The Higher Education Act of 2008 calls for expanded college access for students with intellectual disabilities through comprehensive transition and postsecondary programs. A major focus of the Higher Education Act is the need to develop postsecondary teaching strategies and curriculum consistent with the Universal Design for Learning (UDL).

Autism Spectrum Disorders

Diagnosis and Incidence

Autism is a neurodevelopmental disorder of communication, behavior, and cognition. Individuals with autism vary greatly in intellectual ability, extending from those with severe intellectual disabilities through those who are intellectually gifted and talented. The central defining characteristic of autism is a distinctive impairment in the nature of social communicative development (Bregman & Higdon, 2012). There is an oft repeated saying that if you know one person with autism, you know only one person with autism—highlighting the uniqueness of all individuals, including those on the autism spectrum.

Years ago autism was considered a syndrome; today it is a spectrum disorder. The diagnosis for the autism syndrome and the autism spectrum are similar, and are based on common core characteristics related to communication/language delay or absence; poor social interaction; stereotypic behaviors, such as hand flapping; repetitive verbalizations and behaviors; and restricted interests. These symptoms have remained mainstays of the diagnostic criteria. Interestingly, while scientific research has provided evidence to support interventions (e.g., applied behavior analysis, TEACCH structured teaching, Greenspan's FloorTime), science has failed to provide answers regarding underlying causes of autism. Mystery surrounds the disorder's increased incidence and etiology.

Autism spectrum disorder has been classified under the umbrella term of pervasive developmental disorders, which include autistic disorder, Asperger syndrome, pervasive development disorder—not otherwise specified, Rhett's disorder, and childhood disintegrative disorder (Adreon & Durocher, 2007). This definition is likely to be somewhat revised in the soon to be released *Diagnostic and Statistical Manual V* (expected 2013), with Asperger syndrome being eliminated as a separate ASD.

Characteristics of College Students with Autism Spectrum Disorders

Students with autism spectrum disorders are not new to college campuses, but the increased number of these students is new.

Throughout modern history, individuals that were most assuredly on the spectrum have attended college and have contributed to society. As identification of students with ASD on campuses has increased, concerns have emerged as to how their communication and behavioral differences may affect the learning environment for other students.

The following pages discuss and explain some of the more commonly seen characteristics of young adults with autism. Much of the information presented has been obtained from reviewing literature and research, while some has been gleaned from observations of various college support programs and should be viewed as anecdotal observations. The most important disclaimer here is that all people are unique to themselves, and so each individual with autism is exactly that—an individual unique unto him/herself.

Some of the more salient characteristics of ASD will be described and explained with regard to how they impact learning and participation in college courses. This introductory section explains several types of challenges facing students with ASD so that they may be addressed with the strategies and supports described later in the manual. Note that language processing, social communication, executive functioning, and sensory integration are explained in more detail in chapter 2 in the context of students' learning needs. Before reading the following chapters, it is recommended that instructors take time to digest and reflect upon the characteristics described so that strategies are more likely to be implemented successfully.

Social Interaction

Young adults with autism are often less socially and emotionally mature than their neurotypical counterparts. Impairment in social reciprocity is a central trait of adolescents on the spectrum, with difficulty in the give and take of social interaction. In particular, we see a difference in students with ASD from students with neurotypical development in their integration of verbal and nonverbal social conversation (Bregman & Higdon, 2012). Individuals with ASD often have difficulty with comprehension and appreciation of subtle emotional states within themselves and others, as well as the ability to predict thoughts, feelings, and reactions of other persons (Bregman & Higdon, 2012). Naivety and vulnerability are common concerns among parents and caregivers of individuals in this age-group, even when students are highly intelligent. Often, these students lack guile, being far too honest and blunt. Sometimes their matter-of-factness and bluntness give the impression that they are arrogant. Most usually, this is far from the case and they are puzzled by other people's reaction to their honesty. These students have grown up with different socialization experiences than their peers. They have had fewer opportunities to explore meaningful relationships with peers of either their own or opposite gender, resulting in less reinforcement of appropriate behaviors. In short, personal relationships, etiquette rules, and boundaries are enigmatic.

Students of college-age often state a desire to have friends and may speak bitterly about the loneliness and isolation that they experience in their daily lives. Yet, when friendly advances are directed toward them, they tend to withdraw—eliminating the possibility of a shared experience and leaving a frustrated and/or hurt person at the other end of the exchange. Individuals with ASD are their own worst enemy in the friendship arena. Even when they share interests with another person, they have difficulty conversing socially about their interests. They may speak at length about a topic with seeming disregard for the listener's interest; and although they may actually prefer having dinner with someone rather than eating alone, students often report that they bring their meals back to their room. Left to their own initiative, most college-age youth with ASD are unlikely to initiate appropriate social contact.

While extending an invitation to another student to engage in a shared activity appears to be difficult for many young adults on the spectrum, when opportunities are available and they are encouraged to engage, we have found that many students enjoy the company of their peers. We have observed that in group events, students often remain following the event because they hunger for company in a nonthreatening, socially safe environment.

But then again, the staff hears frequently from students that they do not wish to be part of a group. Much of this attitude is directly related to an aversion to being labeled as a "special needs person." Some students with ASD have difficulty with group participation of any kind. It is helpful to plan activities related to particular interests and then to treat the students with the same respect given to other college-age young adults, by encouraging, not enforcing participation.

In group settings, social communication can be problematic. It is often difficult for students with ASD to process fast-paced abstract social language, especially in lecture-style classes. Because they may miss subtle points and key themes, a response may be seemingly unrelated to the conversation. When surveyed about their social conversational skills, however, they often describe themselves as more competent than their assessment scores indicate (Zager & Alpern, 2010).

College faculty who understand these social and communication challenges can provide a positive environment for participation and growth for their students with ASD. Students who are shy, withdrawn, or inappropriately enthusiastic may be channeled proactively by a knowledgeable professor. Strategies for engaging diverse learners and empowering everyone to actively participate in social conversations and activities in class are provided in the upcoming sections of the manual.

Executive Functioning

Executive functions are processes that permit individuals to manage themselves, their activities, and their resources in order to achieve goals. They have been likened to a complicated Global Positioning System for the brain (Azano & Tuckwiller, 2011) that can help guide the individual through unfamiliar territory and/or help one to stay on track when navigating through a project. Neurologically based skills involving emotional control and self-regulation fall under the umbrella of executive functioning.

Executive dysfunction can result in students having difficulty following a lecture and staying "tuned in." They become easily distracted and begin doing an unrelated task during a class without realizing that their attention has drifted. Or in a science laboratory class that requires following many step-by-step instructions, there may be difficulty transitioning to the next step and staying on task. At such times, other classmates may think the student with ASD is uninterested, incapable, or downright lazy. But given the needed support to stay on track, these students may be the ones to discover the best solution to the lab problem.

Noise and conflicting activities can elevate executive dysfunction. The presence of too many conflicting stimuli tends to be unsettling for students with ASD. Also, anxiety and agitation significantly increase executive dysfunction. College students with ASD find it especially difficult to manage their time, structure and organize their day, fulfill obligations and responsibilities, get to classes and meetings punctually, pace themselves in long-term assignments, organize written work, maintain focus, and so on. They do not intend to be irresponsible. In fact, they most likely would be pleased to meet obligations better. Aids and supports can work miracles in helping students with ASD to manage their lives. Planner books, online calendars, and time alarms, among other tools, were made to order for this group of individuals.

Information Processing

Processing includes the ability to register, decode, and comprehend abstract patterns and sequences. In the absence of comprehension, development cannot move forward (Weider, 2012). Information processing involves (a) taking new data into the brain; (b) sorting out the data so that it can be anchored to existing data and therein make sense; (c) filing the understood information in the brain so that it may be retrieved at a later time; and (d) encoding the information for expression. Breakdowns in information processing may occur in one or a combination of these steps.

Sitting in a college lecture-style class with a professor who is speaking in sophisticated abstract language can be extremely difficult. If the professor is speaking rapidly to cover a large range of new material, presenting information in a disorganized fashion, or jumping from topic to topic, students with ASD tend to become anxious and distracted. In such cases, they may not hear or understand necessary information.

Further, changes in assignments and assessment requirements may be difficult to understand if they are communicated spontaneously and verbally, rather than in writing on the course syllabus. How is the student who is still trying to understand the abstract language (because he/she thinks in literal language) supposed to follow the lecture while simultaneously writing notes, and asking questions? This is where note takers and assistive technology enter the picture. These accommodations are explained in detail in the next section of this chapter.

Sensory Issues

Hyper and/or hypo-sensitivity to sensory input are well-documented in case studies of individuals with autism. Inability to adequately modulate sensory input produces disordered perceptions of external events and results in unusual responses to sensory stimuli (Tsatsanis, 2005). The ability to tolerate and properly register sensory stimuli, whether touch, sound, smell, vision, or movement in space, is affected in many individuals who have autism.

In classrooms, there is an array of variables that can cause sensory discomfort and result in agitation or inattention. Specifically, these might include fluorescent lighting that flickers or buzzes, the hum of air conditioning or cold air blowing, noise outside the classroom, a fellow student sneezing or coughing, movements of other students, or a professor that continuously clears his/her throat. Students with ASD may need to scout out the classroom and find the best place to sit, which may be near the door in case they need a break from the irritating stimuli.

Comorbid Features

Neurodevelopmental disorders seldom appear in isolation. Rather they are often observed to exist in combination with other conditions, which can aggravate the primary symptoms. Conditions frequently associated with autism include anxiety, attention disorders, disordered thinking, and depression. Anxiety and attention disorders are described in more detail below.

ANXIETY.   As children with ASD mature, anxiety tends to increase (Bregman & Higdon, 2012). In addition, the degree of anxiety experienced has been correlated with cognitive functioning (White, Oswald, Ollendick, & Scahill, 2009), indicating that academically talented or gifted college students may present with a significantly higher incidence of debilitating anxiety. Higher levels of anxiety are seen when students become overwhelmed by unpleasant sensory stimulation or when they experience feelings of loss of control. As these feelings escalate, depression may be the result. An awareness of failure to establish relationships, make friends, or participate as part of a group has been connected to onset of depression (Klin, McPartland, & Volkmar, 2005).

We have witnessed students whose anxiety levels have caused their primary disability to intensify. For example, a student with Asperger syndrome and dyslexia looses the ability to read questions and write answers when he became anxious in a testing situation. Another student with high-functioning autism finds it impossible to write essays when anxious. Yet when provided with a reader and scribe, both of these students are able to consistently score nearly perfect papers.

In a different situation involving anxiety, a student became tense and agitated by coughing in his classroom. The sensory discomfort caused by the coughing lowered his ability to concentrate, which in turn caused him to become anxious that he was missing important information. As his sensory discomfort from the coughing and his anxiety increased, he turned and inappropriately insulted the person that was coughing. In an attempt to control his anxiety in situations such as this, his coach is working with him to develop a strategy to self-edit his behavior through cognitive behavioral intervention. It is especially interesting to note that this young man exhibits excellent insight into the causes and consequences of his behavior after the behavior has occurred; but he has limited ability to self-regulate at the time of the affront.

ATTENTION DEFICIT DISORDER (ADD).   For a variety of reasons (e.g., sensory discomfort, anxiety, information processing challenges) students with ASD may exhibit attention disorders. When professors observe students turning their back to the front of the room, answering cell phones, dozing in class, or drawing pictures, they are apt to find such behavior inappropriate, disrespectful, or disturbing. Often times, however, these behaviors are survival mechanisms for students with ASD. We have found it helpful to advise students to take a short break and leave the classroom when they feel exhausted or overwhelmed to the point that they are unable to sit and concentrate. The key to this strategy is to help students become aware of their feelings and to provide a mnemonic for reminding them of the strategy.

Blips and Snowballs

We often come face to face with students who feel defeated. It is not uncommon for students to become agitated because of what they perceive as a major unsolvable problem. While causes of the problems vary, the behavior pattern exhibited nearly every time has become familiar. First, the student experiences a problem, usually due to executive dysfunction. This could be not completing an assignment, misplacing a piece of equipment, missing a class, or having an altercation with an authority figure, as some examples. Next, while being "stuck" worrying about the problem and incapable of correcting the mishap, the student may miss other deadlines, which compounds the initial problem. For instance, a film major lost a camera and stayed awake most of the night worrying about how to tell his parents and feeling guilty about the expense incurred. He finally fell asleep at 5 am, and then missed his English class in the morning because he overslept. He was now afraid that his grade in the missed class would be lowered. When he was informed that the camera had been located and that he would not be penalized for the missed class, he became depressed because he felt that he was continually messing up. It took some time to recover from the depression and to get back on track.

Or, a student studied diligently for an English exam. She determined that she would try to take the exam in her class rather than using a distraction-free setting. In the class, she was unable to respond to any questions. She felt so badly that even though she was permitted to take the exam the next day in a special setting—and even though she knew all the answers—she could not respond to the questions because she was still reliving the perceived mistake of trying to take the exam with her classmates.

In short, moving forward from unsuccessful situations is extremely difficult for students with ASD. Perceived failures build on each other and often lead to episodes of depression. Negative disordered thinking takes precedence over optimism. However, we have also witnessed success building upon success. It seems the key ingredient to progress is for the educator to identify accomplishments and to continually increase awareness and appreciation of true successes, using these to pave the path toward further achievements.

The Role of Colleges and Universities

Accommodations

Students with disabilities are entitled to educational accommodations to enable them to learn and compete in school. Frequently utilized accommodations include extended test time and/or testing in a quiet setting, note takers, readers and/or scribes, and assistive technologies. It is up to the student to self-advocate for accommodations and it is the responsibility of colleges and universities to comply with the law to help enhance college success for all students. The Office for Disabilities at every university is responsible for assuring compliance with Section 504 of the Rehabilitation Act and providing needed accommodations. The office must also be sure to avoid providing undocumented accommodations that could give an unneeded and unfair advantage for any student.

Test Setting and Time Allotted

Due to a variety of reasons (e.g., physical motor challenges, information processing, expressive language challenges), students may require more time to take tests. Because college exams may be very complex and take hours to complete, sometimes a test must be broken into sections for students. Students that received time-and-a-half in high school and used all their allotted time, may require double time for college tests. This is because of the complex nature of college tests and the degree of abstract and conceptual reasoning required.

In order to reduce distractions, students may take exams in separate distraction-free settings. This is especially helpful for students with sensory issues and those with ADD. It is also necessary for students who require readers or scribes. It is the college student's responsibility to request these accommodations. If the documentation supports their request, the Office for Disabilities will help find a suitable setting to take exams. It is sometimes advisable to provide separate distraction-free test settings and test administrators because (a) they may be knowledgeable about particular students' needs, (b) students are familiar with the coaches, and (c) anxiety may, therefore, be effectively controlled. It is possible to provide needed support with sufficient guidance without diluting the integrity of the exam.

Note Takers

Students with ASD may have learning differences that involve information processing and often dysgraphia, or illegible handwriting. Note takers can provide a valuable service by giving the student a set of class notes after each class. Usually, students take their own notes in addition to the note taker and then compare their notes after the class to ensure they have an accurate record of the lesson. This permits the student with ASD to focus his/her concentration on the class lecture or activities. Note takers are paid by the university, and often are not informed of the student's name that they are helping. Sometimes, students desire to know their note taker so that they can communicate with them as needed; it is up to the individual student. The role of being a note taker must be presented to the class as a request for an anonymous student, unless otherwise specified.

Occasionally, a professor refuses to help a student obtain the needed support. On one occasion, a math professor actually told a student who had handed him documentation for a note taker that he didn't need a note taker because he wasn't blind. This professor was breaking the law by refusing to help the student that was enrolled in his class. Unfortunately, this professor is not alone. Another professor felt that it was not her responsibility to have a student with autism in her class and stated that we had "inflicted" upon her a student with disabilities but that she wasn't a special education teacher—rather she was an expert in her field and she wanted us to withdraw the student. In both cases, we withdrew the students because a pyrrhic victory would have been at their expense. But this wasn't fair, nor just; the students' rights were denied.

Readers and Scribes

Some students with ASD have learning disabilities that interfere with their test taking performance. In cases in which such a disability can be documented through a neuropsychological evaluation, students may have someone read the test questions for them. Similarly, if they are impaired in their expressive ability, a scribe may be provided. In neither case is the test modified or diluted. Answers are not given, hints are not provided. The student is merely afforded an opportunity to demonstrate his/her knowledge and competence in a fair and equitable manner.

Assistive Technology

Some students with ASD benefit from using various types of assistive technology. Such technology may include, but is not limited to, LiveScribe smartpens, computers, calculators, and Dragon Naturally Speaking voice recognition software. If assistive technology devices have been included in students' individual education plans from high school, they are most likely entitled to continue the use of these devices. Computers are especially useful for students with handwriting and language-based challenges.

Summary

Upon completion of this chapter, faculty should have knowledge about legislation regarding students' educational rights and college/professorial responsibilities. In addition, core characteristics of ASD were described and explained, along with some insights into why professors can expect to continue to see increasing numbers of students with disabilities in their classes. The information presented in this chapter was intended to increase awareness and appreciation of who these students are and to develop an understanding of the underlying rationale for various accommodations and how they may be utilized. As readers progress through the manual, strategies for engaging all learners in college classes will be connected to the core challenges of autism.

2

IN THE CLASSROOM

Students with ASD face challenges to learning in various areas. Difficulties in language processing, social communication, organizational skills, and sensory functioning may keep them from achieving their potential and may present challenges to the professors who teach them. This chapter will describe these areas, including how they manifest in the student and why, with strategies to address problems that may arise in class. The strategies presented in this chapter result from application of best practices in the field of ASD and our own experiences, as well as feedback from professors who have taught the students, and the students themselves.

Faculty Perceptions of Students with ASD

A preliminary survey of university faculty who have had students with ASD in their classrooms was constructed to better understand how students with ASD are viewed by their professors. Based on a review of literature in the field (Adams, Green, Gilchrist, & Cox, 2002; Bellon-Harn & Harn, 2006; Brinton, Robinson, & Fujiki, 2004; Capps, Kehres, & Sigman, 1998) and on knowledge of the students with learning differences, a survey of 17 behaviors that faculty might see in a classroom was developed. These behaviors related to learning styles, verbal and nonverbal communication skills, and appropriateness of behavior in the classroom.

Approximately 69 faculty members responded to the questions. While not all students with ASD exhibited all the behaviors, the majority of the behaviors described were observed at least occasionally by the faculty members who responded. Respondents reported observing problems that could be understood in terms of both language and communication deficits and executive functions. Challenges in the area of language and communication included difficulty asking and answering questions in class, monopolizing class discussions, going off topic, and limited comprehension of nuanced, abstract information. Difficulties associated with executive functioning included not understanding alternative points of view, submitting home assignments that did not reflect in-class learning, limited comprehension of complex concepts, distractibility, and chronic lateness or absence. The complete survey with results can be found in Appendix A.

The above behaviors might be interpreted negatively by professors, and students displaying these behaviors may be labeled as rude, uninterested, disorganized, or inattentive. Some behaviors may be interpreted in different ways depending on the situation in which they are exhibited.

Behaviors that may be interpreted as being rude include the following:

- Blunt comments
- Engaging in long monologues

- Perseverating on topics that are of interest only to them
- Interrupting others
- Difficulty considering another person's opinion
- Inappropriate language style when speaking to professors —too familiar or informal
- Inappropriate language style when speaking to peers—too formal
- Talking off topic
- Monopolizing the conversation.

Behaviors that might be interpreted as showing a lack of interest include the following:

- Poor eye contact
- Inappropriate body language, including excessive fidgeting or slumping
- Unusual sounds
- Attention to cell phones or other electronic devices
- Leaving the room frequently
- Not asking questions when they don't understand an assignment
- Not participating in class discussions
- Flat tone of voice
- Poor performance on tests
- Handing in assignments late or incomplete.

Behaviors that may be interpreted as disorganized include:

- Commenting on topics unrelated to the discussion
- Excessive questioning about information that has been covered
- Not completing assignments correctly or on time
- Difficulty completing their share of a group project
- Poorly organized research papers

- Showing up late for class
- Excessive absences.

Behaviors that may be interpreted as inattentive that are associated with executive function include:

- Asking questions unrelated to the class discussion
- Asking questions that have already been answered.

Understanding the nature of ASD can help professors interpret the above behaviors in a more useful way, which can lead to more effective strategies for helping these students succeed. Both language/communication deficits and weak executive functioning can combine to result in the behaviors listed above. We will examine many of these behaviors, first from the perspective of language and communication deficits, and then from the perspective of executive functioning.

Learning Needs and Challenges of Students with ASD

Language Processing and Social Communication

Difficulty in the use of language for social purposes is a defining characteristic of autism spectrum disorders (Bregman & Higdon, 2012). Research has shown that although communication skills improve as children with ASD mature (Alpern & Zager, 2007; Howlin, Mawhood, & Rutter, 2000), language problems persist into adulthood and may interfere with communicative interactions between the student and his/her professors, peers, and employers (Zager & Alpern, 2010). Students with autism spectrum disorders may experience difficulty in college classrooms where language-based behaviors such as discussions, group projects, and questioning are encouraged.

Although college-aged students with autism generally speak clearly, in well-formed sentences with age-appropriate vocabulary, they may lack knowledge or awareness of the unwritten social rules for both verbal and nonverbal communication. These students can appear to be rude, uninterested, inattentive, or disorganized in their behavior. While students without ASD may also exhibit these behaviors, the quality and quantity of these behaviors can make the student with ASD stand out. Furthermore, some students with ASD occasionally exhibit unusual nonverbal behaviors that may alienate both the professor and the other students.

To understand the source of the communication problems sometimes seen in young adults with ASD, it is helpful to examine the core characteristics of the disorder. One of these is variously referred to as joint attention, perspective taking, or theory of mind (Baron-Cohen, Leslie, & Frith, 1985; Wetherby, Prizant, & Schuler, 2003; Woods & Wetherby, 2003). Other core characteristics are use of symbols and auditory processing.

Theory of Mind

Even before babies can speak, they communicate through body language. By 12 months, most infants show some joint attention (Toth, Munson, Meltzoff, & Dawson, 2006). They use alternating eye contact and can follow the gaze and point of others. Babies who do not attend to what their caregivers are saying or do not try to engage caregivers through pointing and eye contact, are said to have limited joint attention. These infants and toddlers show late language development and are often later identified as having ASD (Anderson et al., 2007; Charman, Baron-Cohen, Swettenham, Baird, Drew, & Cox, 2003). Although many eventually learn to speak, they continue to show difficulty with communication. Limitations in joint attention lead to an inability to take the listener's perspective into account.

The term "theory of mind" has been used to describe the ability to relate to and make sense of the world in which we live. All knowledge, thoughts, beliefs, and desires make up one's individual theory of mind and this process of accumulation begins as early as the age of four. Developing an understanding that others have thoughts, beliefs, and desires that regulate behavior is an important skill for functioning in society. People with ASD have limited capacity for recognizing these differences and therefore do not engage in "joint attention." Competent communicators understand and are aware of what the listener knows, in other words, what is in the listener's mind. Without theory of mind, students with ASD may not give enough background information or possibly repeat information that is already known, making their spoken or written narratives difficult to follow. To effectively participate in a conversation with a peer or in a class discussion, speakers must be sensitive to the interests of others and to the previous knowledge of those involved (Rubin & Lennon, 2004).

Speakers must also be sensitive to the social context. For example, one speaks in a more formal, polite tone to professors; one does not curse or use slang in a classroom; and one takes turns in a discussion. Being unaware of the unwritten social rules of the classroom might lead the students to speak to professors as if they were peers, or alternatively, to address peers in language that is too formal to be conducive to the formation of friendships. When students make blunt comments that may be insensitive to the feelings of others, rather than being "rude" they may be unable to comprehend how their statements might affect others. When they speak for too long or talk only on topics of interest to themselves, they may be unable to keep the interests of others in mind.

Furthermore, students with ASD may have difficulty reading the body language of listeners that normally gives one cues that the listener is bored or uncomfortable. Additionally, their own body language may not imply anything about their interest level in the topic but instead reflects a habitual difficulty demonstrating an acceptable listening attitude; that is, sitting a little forward, nodding in agreement, and making sufficient eye contact. Many college-aged students with ASD are aware of their difficulties communicating in a group setting with their peers. They may experience anxiety about speaking in situations where the other participants are unfamiliar to them. Their body language may actually discourage the professor from calling on them. Sitting in the back of the room and avoiding eye contact sends a message that "I am not interested."

Tone of voice may also be used to gauge interest level. The monotone of voice seen in some students with ASD may be interpreted as showing lack of enthusiasm. An alternative interpretation relates to theory of mind. Competent speakers vary the intensity of individual words or phrases in order to highlight information on which the listener needs to focus. A simple sentence such as "The boy wants to eat," changes meaning if the stressed word is "boy" or if the stressed word is "eat." Word stress is an unconscious way to make a point clearer to the listener. Speakers who are not focused on listener needs may have little understanding of word stress and therefore speak in a rather "flat" or monotone way (Church, Alisanski, & Amanullah, 2000; Shriberg et al., 2001).

Symbol Use

A second important characteristic of ASD seen from infancy relates to the use of symbols (Prizant, Wetherby, Rubin, & Laurent, 2003; Wetherby et al., 2000). Symbol use is essential for the development of conventional communication, both verbal and nonverbal. Symbolic nonverbal behaviors in infancy include the use of familiar gestures such as waving bye-bye and playing appropriately with toys. The appearance of words to communicate is dependent on symbolic function because words are symbols which represent concepts. The pretend play seen in preschoolers is also a form of early symbolic behavior. Symbols are used to represent more abstract concepts as language skills mature.

The development of both language and play skills are delayed in children with ASD. High-functioning individuals with autism eventually develop age-appropriate language skills but young adults with ASD may continue to have difficulties when dealing with the higher levels of abstract language required for both academic and social success. Areas of concern may include understanding and using sarcasm, humor, and other forms of nonliteral language (e.g., idioms, metaphors, slang). The tendency to interpret information concretely may compromise analytic tasks such as the ability to consider alternative points of view. Classroom discussions are fast-paced, abstract, filled with figurative and nonliteral references, and as described above, dependent on the ability to take another's perspective. College-level textbooks are filled with abstract, nuanced material. Such advanced language skills can be weak even in academically competent individuals with ASD (Bellon-Harn & Harn, 2006; Brinton et al., 2004; Capps et al., 1998; Paul, Orlovski, Marchinko, & Volkmer, 2009). Difficulties in use of nonliteral language might account for a student's reticence to ask questions and to participate in classroom discussions and group projects.

Auditory Processing

Another factor that should be considered when trying to understand the language and communication challenges of students with ASD is that some have problems with auditory processing (Wetherby et al., 2000). This means that they have difficulty learning through the auditory modality. Without visual supports, these students may find it difficult to follow lectures and discussions. The rapid flow of language in a lecture may leave them lost early on, so that points which build upon earlier information are not comprehended. Therefore, they cannot formulate specific questions about what they do not understand. If instructions, due dates, and changes in assignments are not provided in a clearly written visual format, classroom requirements may be missed, and the student may appear lost and disorganized when completing assignments. Organizational skills are discussed further in the next section of this chapter.

Executive Functioning and Sensory Integration

Complicated connections exist between ASD, communication, executive functioning, and sensory integration.

While there are many definitions of executive functioning, most researchers agree that it describes a set of skills necessary to complete day-to-day tasks such as planning, organizing, prioritizing, and multi-tasking (Hughes, Russell, & Robbins, 1994; McEvoy, Rogers, & Pennington, 1993; Ozonoff, Pennington, & Rogers, 1991; Russell, Jarrold, & Hood, 1999). In combination with the communication difficulties noted above, limited executive functioning skills contribute to disorganized communication. Students with ASD might have trouble staying on topic, sequencing spoken messages, or writing cohesively because of executive functioning difficulties. As a result of these complicated connections, students with ASD are often rigid, concrete thinkers, lacking flexibility.

Executive functioning is necessary for goal-directed behavior and includes the ability to initiate and end actions within an expected timeframe, to plan future behavior, and to organize thoughts and actions in the face of novel tasks and situations. Executive functioning guides the performance of such activities as planning, organizing, strategizing, paying attention to details, sustaining attention to and remembering details, and managing time and space. These activities require intact attention, memory and motor skills which are often lacking in students with autism. The limited executive functioning skills of students with ASD can impact their ability to control and regulate many of the language, social, and functional behaviors necessary for success in the classroom. Limited control results in poor social interaction because of problems understanding unwritten social rules.

Sensory integration, also referred to as sensory processing, is the ability to simultaneously process the external and internal information with which we are constantly bombarded. Intact sensory processing allows us to participate in daily life. It is intact sensory processing that enables us to enjoy the movies, ride the subway, or multi-task (Miller & Lane, 2000). Students with ASD for whom this integration is difficult may overreact or under-react to visual, tactile, and/or auditory information. It may be difficult for students with sensory processing difficulty to listen to a lecture in a classroom if there is competing noise. Students with sensory integration issues may also have difficulty understanding personal space or processing information that is presented in multiple modalities.

Executive functioning affects the ability to anticipate outcomes and to adapt to the ever-changing world of the classroom. Thus, while college students with autism are often capable of understanding complex concepts it may be challenging when they are asked to organize that information and relate it to past knowledge. These students may perform well on basic tasks of attention but will have difficulty with tasks that require divided or alternating attention. Students for whom sensory processing is an issue will also have difficulty sustaining attention, particularly in a noisy classroom or one that does not have an explicit organizational structure. Answering in class may be challenging for students with auditory processing and organizational difficulties because of the on-the-spot demand for a reply. Having time to organize their thoughts is required. How information is presented, received, and processed is related to three factors in executive functioning and sensory integration: context, instructional pace, and central coherence.

Context

To fully describe the impact of executive functioning and sensory processing on classroom performance it is necessary to understand the relationship between environment and behavior in the student with ASD. Many researchers have described the relationship between ASD and executive functioning in terms of the disconnect between mental operations that allow changes in behavior and the context in which behavior occurs (Miller & Cohen, 2001; Miller & Wallis, 2009). Students with executive dysfunction often are not able to adapt their responses to differing contexts. In the classroom, students with ASD may respond to a variety of situations, information, instructions, questions, and so on with a single learned behavioral response. Limited flexibility in response and rigidity may also prevent a student from adapting to changes in the physical, verbal, and nonverbal environments, factors that must be considered instructionally. In the classroom, this is manifested when students exhibit difficulty following complex instructions (oral and written) due to a limited understanding of the context of those instructions and the communication style of the professor. Students with ASD have a difficult time shifting from one context to the next and often cannot process the change in style, content vocabulary, or linguistic complexity between professors.

Instructional Pace

When students are presented with novel information, they are required to store that information in memory and connect it to previous learning. Students with ASD may respond slowly or require a slower presentation of information because of executive function limitations. Inefficient access to prior knowledge, limited thought organization, impaired self-regulation, attention, and rigidity are factors affecting the pace in which information is processed. The feedback loop required in processing and responding to the variable pace of information, limited working memory associated with executive function, and the varied contexts in which a student must learn can become overloaded, resulting in confusion and frustration.

Central Coherence

Students with ASD are described in the literature as having difficulty seeing the big picture. This skill, known as central coherence, is related to the ability to hold onto information (memory) in order that it may be used to affect future responses. People with intact abilities in this realm get the gist of things because they are able to take information from a variety of sources and/or experiences and create alternate meaning (Frith, 1989). Students with ASD for whom central coherence is not intact are more likely to misinterpret situations and information. Since central coherence also enables us to analyze components of a task and prioritize actions, it is related to executive function skills. Without the ability to make logic of the world students with ASD often use repetitive, learned behaviors and may have heightened sensory perceptions. In addition, students with poor central coherence cannot hold onto one piece of information and move onto the next step in a sequence. Students with ASD approach situations in a detail-oriented fashion often through one sensory modality at a time. This is related to difficulty filtering out stimuli and integrating sensory information. Given difficulty with central coherence or limited capacity to store and retrieve information from memory, these students will need information presented in more than one modality. The student with ASD does not see the "whole" and therefore needs to see that these details are related to the "big picture," for example, the assignment.

Making connections to the texts used in the classroom can be difficult for students with ASD due to lack of central coherence. It is helpful to focus on major events, ideas, and concepts that occur often throughout the lecture, using text markers to engage this connection. It is also useful to incorporate the background information students give about themselves in class so that you can identify connections between them and lecture/text information. Text-to-text connections can be made using charts to compare and contrast important conceptual information. These charts are beneficial in that students with ASD, who have difficulty understanding abstract concepts, can "see" connec-tions. It is important to discuss these connections based on the books/texts assigned in your class and to engage students in a discussion of connections between those books and books they have read outside of class (or in other classes). Text-to-world connections are complicated for ASD students who often see the world from a narrowed perspective. World issues and events are often discussed but not connected in such a way as to help the student with ASD see alternatives to their own thinking. In English classes, for example, bringing awareness to the fact that characters (in books and in reality) are in conflict with social issues will help make these connections more explicit.

In the Classroom and Beyond

For students with ASD, language processing, communication, executive functioning, and sensory processing limitations present challenges that can impact their learning and the development of social relationships in the classroom and beyond, for example, in the workplace. As colleges prepare students for life there is a need to understand the role that language, communication, executive function, and sensory processing play as those skills needed to be successful in the classroom are important for success in life generally. Success in college and in the workplace depends as much on the ability to solve problems, work collaboratively, abide by professional etiquette, and other such noncontent skills referred to as soft skills. These soft skills are particularly challenging for students with ASD. The following soft skills are helpful in facilitating learning and engagement in college:

- **Networking.** Communicating beyond one's inner circle, developing relationships;
- **Enthusiasm.** Taking on other perspectives, understanding and supporting a wide range of interests, taking initiative;
- **Professionalism.** Understanding audience needs, adapting communication style, reflecting workplace etiquette, managing time;
- **Communication skills.** Communicating ideas in an organized, audience-responsive style, understanding timing and attitude when communicating;

- **Teamwork.** Working on projects that require collaboration, knowing how and when to lead, taking on other perspectives, building consensus, communicating;
- **Problem solving and critical thinking.** Using facts, data, and knowledge to solve problems, understanding the big picture.

It is evident that with the increased number of students with ASD entering college and the workplace, postsecondary faculty must expand their knowledge and instructional strategy to meet the needs of students for whom communication and executive functioning skills are limited.

We know that laws relating to the education of students with disabilities raise concerns for postsecondary faculty. The Higher Education Act of 2008, which calls for improved postsecondary education, brings with it the need for university faculty to understand strategy-based instructional methodologies. Students with ASD who have benefitted from inclusive legislation come to college campuses with a list of accommodations that support their diverse learning. These can be as varied as having extra time on exams; using specialized technology for note taking, reading, and speaking; or having an in-class scribe. They are designed to help students with challenges in auditory processing, organizational skills, sensory issues, or anxiety. While these accommodations meet some of the needs of students with disabilities, they may not be sufficient to maximize the learning potential of these students. The purpose of the next section of this manual is provide faculty with strategies that can be used to help these students succeed.

Strategies for Effective Teaching

The first part of this section of the manual describes strategies that professors can utilize to organize and prepare their courses and lectures. Included in this section are teaching techniques related to the Universal Design for Learning (Rose, Harbour, Johnston, Daley, & Abarbanell, 2008) (see Appendix B for UDL descriptors).While these strategies are necessary for students with ASD, they are also useful for all learners. Professors who have had students with disabilities in their classroom have reported that teaching these students makes them better teachers overall. The second part of this section addresses specific problems that may occur while teaching and which may require on-the-spot responses.

Organizing and Preparing the Classroom

1. Use Multiple Methods to Engage Students in the Curriculum

Classroom instruction that presents information relevant to students engages them with a hook that keeps them invested in the process of learning. This requires that professors gain an understanding of what is meaningful to the students and incorporate this into instruction. Providing students with feedback (assessment) and increasing the relevance of the topic for students fosters engagement in the learning process.

It is important to engage all students, but particularly those with ASD, in making connections to text, others, and the world as it is not easy for students with ASD to activate knowledge they have learned previously.

2. Present Information in Multiple Formats

The purpose of providing a variety of means for conveying information is to increase comprehension as well as to engage the learner in the process. Analyze the way in which you present information to your students. In most university settings information is text dominant. Thus, students with ASD are at an immediate disadvantage if they have difficulty processing text, if the language of the text is confusing or complex, or if the text cannot adequately represent the concept being presented. It is important to consider alternative means of presenting the information for those students who have difficulty in a single mode of presentation. The use of illustrations, simulations, tables, models, graphics, and the wide array of internet broadcasting sites, such as YouTube, will enhance engagement and comprehension, therefore improving the student performance.

An important component of the UDL approach to instruction is the use of multiple media as a means of engaging students. Multi-media presentations range from the simple (e.g., graphic organizers, charts, handouts) to complex technological applications (e.g., text to speech software such as Kurzweil). Depending on your specific classroom you may have the opportunity to provide students with this entire range—visual and audio. Visual supports may improve students' comprehension. Providing information visually, for example via charts, lists, and diagrams, will facilitate visual memory for recalling information. Similarly, audio supports can engage students in the process of listening for improved auditory processing. Some students may find it more engaging to listen to the text or listen to instructions on an audio-recording rather than reading them. For example, a downloadable app available on the iPad allows recordings to be made on the spot.

3. Prepare Students Before the Semester Begins

Most universities have online student sites, such as Blackboard, where information can be made available before the semester even begins. Providing the syllabus with the required textbooks and course requirements will be helpful. Including office hours and professor contact information on the syllabus may encourage students to ask questions and develop a relationship early on. Giving students a clear calendar of due dates for assignments and/or homework without visually overwhelming them will allow students to plan their time accordingly and increase the likelihood of their success in your course. Should any changes in schedule and/or routine be necessary, preparing students with ASD in advance will be important.

4. Prepare Students Before Each Class

Weekly reminders about topics that will be covered in class will allow students to ask better questions in class, to participate more comfortably in group discussion, and to follow the information with greater understanding. Professors may want to provide students with a copy of their lecture notes, or alternatively they may post an outline or a PowerPoint of the lecture online, which is a popular option. Students both with and without disabilities may need to be reminded to download these notes, read them before class, and bring a copy to the lecture. These reminders should also be provided in a visual format, not just verbally. Additionally, should professors wish to provide students with information before the day of each class, they might want to consider providing a weekly chart that clearly outlines expectations or a detailed description of daily assignments, depending on the course. These visual charts can be used for homework/class assignments and will reduce the amount of

Table 2.1 Visual Supports for Assignments

WEEK	DATE OF CLASS	TOPIC	READING REQUIRED FOR CLASS

Class discussion:

Assignment:

incorrectly completed assignments. Students with ASD, and others, will benefit from checklists, charts, and other visual supports that they can cross-reference and cross out when completed.

5. Prepare Students for Papers and Exams

Exam dates and project/paper due dates should be reviewed frequently, especially if changes have been made in either the date or the content of any assignment. Any changes should be announced both verbally and in a written format. Providing sample exam questions, review sheets, or sample papers will help students complete assignments and respond to exams more effectively. Both the content and structure of written work can be improved through incorporating the practice of requiring first drafts which are returned with feedback.

6. Design Exams, Handouts, and PowerPoint Slides to be User-friendly

In an exam, students will be better able to recall information when test items are constructed in a style that is consistent with the way information was presented in class. Grouping related items together will also help in the retrieval process. Concise and well-organized handouts that highlight key points can structure and reinforce content. If using PowerPoint in class, keep the information on each slide to a minimum and use a font size that can be read from the back of the room. Implicit information should be stated explicitly so that students make the important connections that will result in complete, coherent assignments. Since students on the spectrum often need visual supports it is recommended that significant due dates (e.g., for projects, long-term assignments, quizzes) are shown in bold, highlighted, and/or underlined. This gives the student a framework for planning and executing the required work. It will also be beneficial to that student's support personnel and/or disabilities counselor who can help with continued organization.

7. Structure the Lesson

Thinking about the organizational structure of the lesson will support all students in their learning. Simple methods of organizing the class include: using the same space each day (blackboard, Smartboard, etc.) when writing down assignments; beginning the lecture with a preview statement, such as "In today's lecture you will learn about . . ."; ending the lecture with a review statement, such as "Today you learned that . . ."; or asking students to relate one concept they understood from the lecture. These strategies alert the learner to expectations and are important tools for ensuring that students do not comment on topics unrelated to the lecture.

8. Provide Visual Organizers/Templates

Using graphics to represent or organize information provides students with ASD a visual strategy that can improve note taking and comprehension, and enhance engagement. Simple charts and graphs can be given out to all students at the beginning of the semester and/or weekly depending on the course requirements. They become useful resources for engaging students in a lecture, for students to use as review for assessment, and as planning tools for any writing requirement. Table 2.2 and Figure 2.1 are two examples of visual organizers.

Students can be given a simple Compare/Contrast Chart to list the information that is provided in a lecture. The lecturer can verbally alert them to important concepts during the lecture by saying such things as, "The first important concept to remember is . . . ." An assignment then might be to compare and contrast these concepts for the topic discussed. This exemplifies how a visual organizer can be used to solidify knowledge for students with memory and auditory processing difficulties.

A Problem/Solution Chart can be used to support students who have difficulty taking perspective and understanding how the details affect the whole (central coherence). Students with ASD can "see" how a problem may have more than one solution and result using such a chart.

Table 2.2 Compare/Contrast Chart

	TOPIC	TOPIC
Important concept 1		
Important concept 2		
Important concept 3		

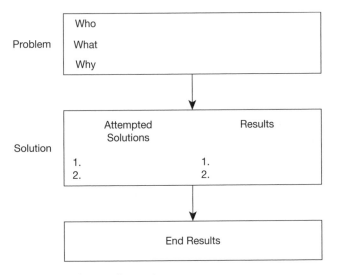

Figure 2.1 Problem/Solution Chart

9. *Prepare Students for Change*

The issue of change as it relates to organization and anxiety is important to understand and can be addressed through simple environmental strategies. Students with ASD need routine and predictability. When changes occur, as they will, students with ASD often do not accept or process them, resulting in limited classroom success. Thus, even a "bright" student who is able to comprehend complex concepts will be thrown by changes in routine, timeframes, scheduling, use of resources, assignments, and so on. A student who expects that a class will end at a certain time may get up and walk out of class at that time! Preparing for change, reviewing the schedule periodically, and notifying students of change in advance will support their success.

One solution is to pair the student with a "buddy" who is willing to review assignment requirements with them. Clearly this strategy would require prior agreement from the student who may be able to suggest someone with whom they feel comfortable enough to ask or allow the professor to ask. It needs to be made clear that the buddy cannot do the work but that he/she is available to review the assignment before it is begun and during its completion.

10. Provide Frequent and Varied Assessment of Performance

Shorter, more frequent exams or quizzes break the information down into more manageable pieces than the traditional midterm plus final exam used in many college classes. Frequent exams/quizzes also allow students more opportunities for feedback about how they are doing in the course and act as study guides for more comprehensive exams. A variety of question types on an exam (essay, multiple choice, true/false, or short answers) will allow students with varied strengths to display their knowledge. Assessment approaches other than in-class exams, such as oral presentations, group projects, case study analyses, and take-home exams will also allow multiple ways to demonstrate learning.

11. Discuss Behavior Standards

Behaviors that are acceptable in university classrooms differ from high school and also differ from professor to professor. It is often assumed that students are aware of these standards, but those unwritten "rules" are often unclear to students without disabilities as well as those with disabilities. Behaviors that might be addressed include what to call the professor, rules for cell phone use, attendance requirements, protocol for answering or asking questions in class, rules for food in class, or when it is permitted to leave the room. Some students may need to be reminded if class participation or punctuality count in the final grade. Other students may need reminders about talking to other students during the lecture. A discussion of what it means to cheat or plagiarize at the university level and the consequences of this should be reviewed at the beginning of the semester, as many universities already ensure. Making this information clear to all students may help eliminate disruptive behaviors before they begin.

12. Reduce Sensory Input

Be aware that students with ASD can have difficulty with background noise, lighting, and/or space. Encourage students to sit away from windows. If the classroom has fluorescent lighting that buzzes it will be important to discuss options with the student for how to best manage this distraction.

13. Reinforce Soft Skill Work

Provide students the opportunity to practice collaboration, problem-solving, and critical thinking skills. Project-based learning methods support engagement and allow students to use important 21st century skills. Allowing students to engage in the process of working in teams with specific roles that are clearly defined will help students with ASD to build relationships and to avoid unnecessary conflict in the collaborative process.

Communication in a peer-group academic setting has a different dynamic than communication with a professor in a lecture or class discussion format. The role of the professor as the leader is clearly established; often it is the professor who sets the topic and regulates who speaks. When students interact in a group project, roles are not as clear. Furthermore, students must take more responsibility and be more creative in communicating to complete the task. Table 2.3 provides a template for possible group members' roles, including Facilitator, Timekeeper, Recorder, and Researcher. Other roles could be assigned depending on the nature of the assignment. If the class is small enough so that a professor knows all the students, roles can be assigned with individual student strengths and weaknesses in mind. A student with ASD may be placed in a group with his/her note taker or "buddy." Initial groups that include students with ASD should be kept to a minimum size.

Students may also need help with suggestions about how to schedule meeting times or ways to communicate. Setting up groups on Blackboard for discussion may be especially helpful to students who are reticent to communicate in person. The use of technology in the creation of collaborative groups will help students with ASD obtain background knowledge before class. Having students share information, questions, and updates on group work via university e-mail is an effective and engaging way for student groups to communicate and it helps the student with ASD break through the social barrier.

Table 2.3 Assigning Specific Roles

FACILITATOR	TIMEKEEPER	RECORDER	RESEARCHER
• Moderates discussion • Ensures participation	• Sets agenda • Keeps members on task	• Takes notes • Prepares conclusion	• Acts as liaison between group and instructor
Topic(s)	Timeframe(s)	Facts/concepts/conclusions	Information needed

Responding to Situations in Class

It is evident from the strategies provided above that a few simple preparatory and regulatory instructional techniques will address a broad range of behaviors associated with classroom response for students with ASD. However, some more specific suggestions for dealing with situations that are frequently encountered by professors in the classroom will also be helpful and are provided here.

1. **What can I do to encourage greater class participation?**
   - Prepare the student by indicating that he/she will be called on to answer a specific question.
   - Wait awhile for students to prepare an answer before calling on anyone.
   - Provide discussion questions before the class and indicate which question(s) will be the responsibility of each student.
   - Write the question on the board. Auditory stimuli are fleeting but the written form of the question remains for students to process in their own time.
   - Use the same spaces on the board for questions and assignments, keeping these areas separate to avoid confusion.
   - Divide the class into groups to discuss a question and allow the students to come up with an answer together. Even if the student with ASD does not actually report the group answer, he/she will have had a successful small group participation experience.
   - Provide specific roles to students during the discussion to facilitate participation.
   - Provide opportunities for online discussions. Many of the quietest students are willing to post their thoughts and opinions online since that is a means of communication

that most students in this age group are completely comfortable with.

- Speak to the student after class about why he/she does not participate and how you can help.

2. What can I do if a student monopolizes the class discussion?

- Respond respectfully with feedback, such as "That's very interesting but Ethan also had his hand up so before class ends, I'd like to give him a chance."
- Develop unobtrusive hand signals that have been agreed upon in advance, such as tapping on the wrist (even if not wearing a wrist-watch), as a cue to help the student become aware that he/she is talking for too long.

3. What can I do if a student frequently answers off topic?

- Use agreed upon hand signals to alert changes in topic.
- Rephrase the question if you think the student has misunderstood.
- Write the question on the board if you have not already.
- Use other students to bring the student back on topic by asking for their feedback.
- Use the topic the student is talking about to open up the discussion to new ideas.

4. What can I do to help a student who becomes restless and fidgety and disturbs the rest of the class?

- Allow use of headphones to reduce extraneous noise.
- Use an FM unit to amplify your voice for the student.
- Provide pre-arranged movement breaks.
- Ensure the student is not seated next to a window or door with background noise. Allow students to doodle during the lecture.
- Discuss noise and movement issues with the student before class.

5. What can I do if a student persistently seems to misunderstand assignments?

- Use charts and/or diagrams for important relational concepts.
- List assignment requirements in order of expected completion.
- Provide explicitly stated information and paraphrase information that is inferred in the assignment wording.
- Establish a "buddy" system in your classroom for peer-mediated learning.
- Give step-by-step instructions.
- Allow for audio recordings of the class lecture.
- Be sensitive to the use of metaphoric language and complex sentence structure.
- Use frequent pauses to allow students time to process information.
- Use templates for organizing instruction.
- Write instructions in a linear manner with limited use of idioms, metaphors, or other figurative language.

6. What can I do if a student persistently asks questions about information just stated?

- Invite other class members to explain the information in another way.
- Suggest that the student make an appointment to see you or e-mail you so you can go over the information without disrupting other students.

7. What can I do if a student is rude to other students or to me?

- Go over university rules and set clear guidelines at the beginning of the semester regarding acceptable forms of address, cell phone use, and rules for class participation.

- Include a discussion of the need to respect each other's learning styles, speech patterns, and cultural differences in your syllabus and/or in the class.

8. What do I do if a student has difficulty working in a group?
- Assign students to roles that have clear responsibilities.
- Provide students with templates for recording their responses.
- Use technology to support group work outside of the classroom.

9. What do I do if a student has difficulty doing an oral project?
- Consider alternative or modified assignments.
- Use other university professionals and resources to give the student extra help in oral presentation skills.
- Encourage the use of PowerPoint or other visual supports.

10. What if a student doesn't ever ask questions when he/she doesn't understand?
- Stop at frequent intervals to ask students to paraphrase.
- Give students time to write questions down before asking orally.
- Provide alternative points of view during discussions.
- Have students list alternative viewpoints in a side-by-side or inter-facing chart format.
- Connect classroom discussions with world issues.
- Connect text information to classroom discussions.

The last question is especially pertinent as it is one of the roles of a liberal arts education to expose young adults to new and expanded points of view. Seeing different points of view may be especially difficult for students with ASD because of their tendency to be concrete and rigid in their thinking. Discussions and assignments that explicitly demonstrate possible alternative philosophies and approaches to problem solving can help to build awareness in students, both with and without disabilities.

Summary

It is evident that with the increased number of students with ASD entering college and the workplace, postsecondary faculty must expand their knowledge and instructional strategies to meet the needs of students for whom communication, executive functioning, and sensory integration skills are limited. Students with ASD present specific challenges within the context of a college environment. The flexible, varied schedule of a typical college day poses problems for students who struggle with executive function. The social realm is difficult for those who cannot organize free time or for those who do not know how to navigate the constantly changing, complex relationship-building process. Deficits in language processing, social communication, organizational skills, and sensory processing impact the learning and social development of students with ASD and may keep them from achieving their potential. Difficulty with communication affects comprehension and problems associated with executive function impact organization and assessment. Thus, while high-functioning adolescents and adults with ASD have tremendous potential, communication and executive function deficits present significant obstacles to social, academic, and vocational success. Issues such as the inability to understand the listener's perspective, use of inappropriate voice patterns, and difficulty interpreting figurative and nonliteral utterances suggest that even the most intellectually capable students may require support and understanding from college faculty and staff.

This chapter outlines the particular challenges to college faculty that are presented by students with ASD, and the supports that can be put in place to help student learning. As professors develop curriculum that is accessible and engaging, they are increasingly being asked to analyze their instruction, embrace technology, and modify the teaching environment to ensure that diverse learners are benefitting from college education. The communication, executive function and sensory integration descriptions of students with ASD are provided to support the expansion of faculty knowledge. The 13 strategies for enhancing the educational environment and the responses to situations in class covered in this chapter will also expand the instructional repertoire of college professors. Faculty will need support to meet the challenges associated with these changes and resources vary from college to college.

A transdisciplinary and collaborative approach by the support team can help ensure student success. As a result of a team approach, professors are not left alone to deal with problems that occur in the classroom. The team member who is assigned to each student will identify him/herself at the beginning of the semester and can be contacted if any problems occur. Furthermore, college students with significant learning challenges, such as ASD, will benefit from coaches who review the syllabus for each course with them and help students organize their time, meet deadlines for papers, and review class notes. Coaches act as mentors and enlist faculty support when necessary, thereby helping to ensure that educational goals are met. An integral part of any college support program is the opportunity to use newly acquired social skills in authentic situations. Authentic learning helps students become aware of the nonverbal cues given by listeners, and of the information their body language sends to listeners.

While changes in instructional techniques, environment, and curriculum will address a broad range of issues associated with students with ASD, they will only be successful with the support, feedback, and ongoing assessment of strategy use found in a collaborative educational community.

3

CASE STUDIES

Two case studies are presented here, describing the student's situation and performance in class, and problems that arose. In each case, the college support team defined goals, then offered strategies and accommodations to resolve the problem. These case studies highlight successful approaches in dealing with challenging situations.

Case Study 1

David was an 18-year-old freshman who graduated from a private, regular education high school with support via a special education resource room. He tested within the normal range for IQ. SAT scores were slightly below the minimum required by the university but his high grade point average allowed him to be admitted to the university. His professor reported that he was polite, on time, and had good attendance. However, he had a rather affectless facial expression and made limited eye contact. The professor interpreted this as typical freshman nervousness. David presented a letter from the Office for Disabilities stating that he was to have a note taker and extra time for exams. The professor had had other students with similar needs and was not uncomfortable with these requests. Problems began to occur as David became more comfortable in the class. He began to volunteer to answer more often and the professor was pleased. David's responses were initially on target but he would gradually begin to ramble on so that it was not easy to follow his point. Furthermore, as he spoke longer and longer, he began to mumble and become somewhat unintelligible. It was clear from their body language that the other students in the class were becoming uncomfortable. The professor did not want to embarrass David or avoid calling on him but he also did not want to let the class go off track.

After consulting with a member of the support team, it was decided that four goals had to be met:

1. The professor needed the class to move forward.
2. David needed to learn to monitor the length of his responses.
3. David needed to learn to organize his responses to target the question asked.
4. David needed to improve his articulation (pronunciation) when giving longer responses.

Strategies and Accommodations

1. The professor used phrases that would not embarrass David, for example, "I like your thinking but there were a lot of hands up and class is almost over"; or, "That was interesting but I'm not sure if I got all of your points;

would someone else like to comment or clarify?"; or, "Could I interrupt you for a minute to write your main points on the board?"

2. When possible, the professor wrote questions on the board.

3. The professor utilized a cue that David had learned in his social communication group to tell him he had been talking too long: a tap on the professor's wrist to represent "time." Another cue was used to signal that he was off topic: a small circling of the hands. David and the professor agreed privately that he would watch for the signals, and the professor agreed to do it very discreetly.

4. The speech-language pathologist observed David in the class to determine what behaviors should be targeted and to document progress.

5. David's speech-language pathologist targeted his articulation skills and role-played classroom discussions.

Outcome

David showed an improvement in his awareness, not only of his tendency to speak for too long and off topic but of his need to monitor his pronunciation. Improved communication skills in the classroom were reported not only by subjective reports from the professor, but also based on classroom observations and documentation by the speech-language pathologist. These observations allowed David to receive feedback for continued improvement. It is also of note that as a result of the professor's changes in teaching strategies, all students were more willing to respond in class.

Case Study 2

Max is a highly intelligent college freshman with a diagnosis of Asperger syndrome. Reported academic strengths include attention to detail, knowledge of facts, a love of books, technological skill, and excellent attendance. He has had many years of support with scheduling, organizing his class notes, and managing long-term projects. Max's accommodations on arrival to college included extended time for tests and use of a calculator.

His grades throughout high school were predictive of a successful college experience. During his first semester in college, Max had difficulty with a number of classes. He would often miss a class, arrive late for class, hand in writing assignments that were not complete or cohesive, not turn in assignments at all, and was failing most of his tests. He had difficulty paying attention and professors reported that he would shout out during lectures (e.g., "I don't get this" or "What are you talking about?"). Classes in which Max was required to work in a group were particularly difficult for Max as he would monopolize the discussion, argue with members, or not participate. Max did not seek help from the Office of Disabilities on campus as, like most entering students with ASD, he was not aware that he had to initiate support. While in high school Max had a very rigid schedule of support services, a structured schedule of classes (i.e., a fixed school day with the same amount of time for each class), and lunch at the same time in the same location. He completed his homework at the same time each day after school. At college, his classes were not sequentially scheduled and not all the same length. He had lengthy breaks during the day.

Max's History professor discussed his poor test performance with him and discovered that while Max could recite all of the facts in the text, he could not apply that knowledge to the types of critical thinking questions posed on the exam. He then encouraged Max to contact the Office of Disabilities and a meeting was held to discuss options for Max.

After consulting with a member of the support team, the following goals were agreed upon:

1. Professors would use a consistent format for assigning homework.
2. Max would improve his focus on group work in class.
3. Max would improve his attendance.

Strategies and Accommodations

1. Max would use his iPad as a scheduler. Two schedules were created: one for daily classes and one for organizing time to complete assignments each day. He would use the alarm reminder for important events and to ensure arrival on time to class.
2. Max's professors would provide him with an outline each week that included reading assignments due, significant points of focus in the reading, and study questions related to the assignments.
3. Max would visit the Office of Disabilities at a regularly scheduled time to review notes, assignments, etc.
4. Max would sit at a desk in the middle of the classroom where background noise was lessened as it was learned that his auditory sensitivity was creating anxiety, which resulted in him calling out.
5. Max used color-coded notebooks for each class and each professor agreed to use the same color highlighter on the Smartboard when writing notes.
6. Professors agreed to write all notes on the left side of the board in their room and all assignments on the right side.

7. When working in collaborative groups, a specific task was assigned to Max that focused on his strength—note taking. His notes would then be discussed with one other member of the group to ensure that the important points were highlighted.
8. For courses in which lengthy written papers were required, Max was provided with templates for outlining notes.
9. Max would be assigned a study-buddy for tests and exams.

Outcome

Max's improvement was dramatic. While he still had difficulty in classes that were primarily lectures, he was no longer late for class and his performance on tests improved. He continues to need technological and visual support as well as understanding of his sensory needs.

4

ANNOTATED RESOURCES

Autism

Organizations and Agencies

Association on Higher Education and Disability (AHEAD)

http://www.ahead.org/

Founded in 1977, AHEAD is a professional membership organization for individuals involved in the development of policy and in the provision of quality services to meet the needs of persons with disabilities involved in all areas of higher education. The association boasts over 2,500 members throughout the world, as well as formal partnerships with 30 regional affiliates and numerous other professional organizations working to advance equity in higher education for people with disabilities. AHEAD provides training to higher education personnel through conferences, workshops, publications, and consultation, while its members represent a diverse network of professionals who actively address disability issues on their campuses and in the field of higher education.

Autism Research Institute (ARI)

http://www.autism.com

ARI is the hub of a worldwide network of parents and professionals concerned with autism. ARI was founded in 1967 to conduct and foster scientific research designed to improve the methods of diagnosing, treating, and preventing autism. ARI disseminates research findings to parents and others worldwide seeking help. ARI publishes the *Autism Research Review International*, a quarterly newsletter covering biomedical and educational advances in autism research.

Autism Society of America

http://www.autism-society.org

Autism Society of America is the leading grassroots autism organization, and is committed to improving the lives of all those affected by autism. It provides information, education, supporting research, programs, and services for the autism community. Through its ongoing public awareness campaign, it provides the latest information regarding treatment, education, research, and advocacy. More than 50,000 members and supporters are connected through a working network of nearly 200 chapters nationwide.

Autism Speaks

http://www.autismspeaks.org/

Autism Speaks is the nation's largest autism science and advocacy organization, dedicated to: funding research into the causes, prevention, treatments, and a cure for autism; raising awareness of autism spectrum disorders; and advocating for the needs of individuals with autism and their families.

Center for Autism and Related Disorders (CARD)

http://www.centerforautism.com

CARD is among the world's largest and most experienced organizations effectively treating children with autism and related disorders. With a network of trained supervisors and therapists, CARD provides individualized services to families throughout the world.

Centers for Disease Control and Prevention (CDC)

http://www.cdc.gov/ncbddd/autism/index.html

This U.S. government website provides up-to-date information on autism spectrum disorder, also known as pervasive developmental disorder, including: facts; screening and diagnosis; resources; treatment; data and statistics; research; articles; and free materials.

Council for Exceptional Children (CEC)

http://www.cec.sped.org/am/template.cfm?section=Home

CEC is an international community of professionals who are the voice and vision of special and gifted education. CEC's mission is to improve, through excellence and advocacy, the education and quality of life for children and youth with exceptionalities and to enhance the engagement of their families. The organization provides the following services: professional development opportunities and resources; 17 divisions for specialized information; journals and newsletters with information on new research findings; effective classroom practices; federal legislation and policies; conventions and conferences; and special education publications.

Cure Autism Now Foundation (CAN)

http://www.cureautismnow.org

CAN is an organization of parents, clinicians, and leading scientists committed to accelerating the pace of biomedical research in autism through raising money for research projects, education, and outreach. The foundation funds research through a variety of programs. There are 10 chapters throughout the USA.

Division on Autism and Developmental Disabilities (DADD)

http://daddcec.org/AboutUs.aspx

DADD is an organization committed to enhancing the quality of life of individuals, especially children and youth, with autism, intellectual disabilities, and other developmental disabilities. The division seeks to further the knowledge base of the field, thus ensuring the continued advancement of positive educational and life outcomes for those with autism and developmental disabilities.

Organization for Autism Research (OAR)

http://www.researchautism.org

OAR focuses on applied research. The mission of applying research to answer questions of daily concern for those living with autism drives each of the goals and objectives that define OAR's programs. This entails the systematic investigation of variables associated with positive outcomes in such areas as education, communication, self-care, social skills, employment, behavior, and adult and community living. In this context, its work extends to issues related to family support, the efficacy of service delivery systems, and demographic analyses of the autism community.

OAR funds pilot studies and research within specific modalities and issues affecting the autism community, primarily for studies whose outcomes offer new insights into the behavioral and social development of individuals with autism with an emphasis on communications, education, and vocational challenges.

Think College

http://www.thinkcollege.net

Think College is an initiative of the Institute for Community Inclusion (ICI) at the University of Massachusetts, Boston. ICI has been a leader in research and training in the area of postsecondary education for people with intellectual and other developmental disabilities for over 10 years. To that end, ICI conducts research, training, and technical assistance for professionals, families, and students related to postsecondary education for individuals with intellectual and other developmental disabilities.

US Autism and Asperger Association (USAAA)

http://www.usautism.org

USAAA provides education, research, support, and solutions through conferences, newsletters, and resources. Its mission is to enhance the quality of life of individuals and their families who are touched by autism. USAAA also publishes the WeeklyNews newsletter.

Books and Journal Articles

Adreon, D. & Durocher, J. (2007). Evaluating the college transition needs of individuals with high-functioning autism spectrum disorders. *Intervention in School & Clinic, 42*(5), 271–279.

Increased attention has been given recently to the needs of students with learning and developmental disabilities who are transitioning from high school to college. This is especially important for students with high-functioning autism spectrum disorders, who are likely to experience significant and unique challenges in adjusting to postsecondary educational settings. After an overview of diagnostic criteria, symptom presentation, and treatment approaches for high-functioning students with ASD, this article discusses the type of difficulties students may encounter across various domains, including socialization, communication, independent daily living skills, academic functioning, and self-advocacy. The article concludes with recommendations for areas to be evaluated and addressed when determining the supports students with high-functioning ASD need to succeed in meeting the organizational, academic, and social demands of college life.

Bork, R., Brown, T., & Wolf, L. (2009). *Students with Asperger syndrome: A guide for college personnel*. Shawnee Mission, KS: Autism Asperger Publishing Co.

For many students with autism spectrum disorders, getting admitted to college is the easy part. Surviving and succeeding can be quite another, as these students transition into a system that is often unprepared to receive them. Accommodating students whose disabilities fall into social and self-regulatory areas is a particular challenge for disability services providers who are not used to reaching out into so many areas of student life. This comprehensive book offers disability services professionals practical strategies for accommodating and supporting students in all phases of college life and beyond.

Cohen, M. & Sloan, D. (2007). *Visual supports for people with autism: A guide for parents and professionals*. Bethesda, MD: Woodbine House, Inc.

This book shows parents and educators how incorporating visual supports while teaching can improve academic performance, behavior, interaction with others, and self-help skills. The authors, both certified behavior analysts, describe the deficits typical of autism—language, memory, temporal sequential skills, attention, motivation, and social skills—and present strategies to use visual supports to address those issues at school and home.

Dillon, M. (2007). Creating supports for college students with Asperger syndrome through collaboration. *College Student Journal*, *41*(2), 499–504.

Although individuals with Asperger syndrome usually possess average or above-average intellectual functioning, they often exhibit significant nonacademic disabilities. These can interfere with their academic performance. Consequently college students with AS often fail. Typical college-level special student supports usually do not address these types of problems. This article describes a collaborative arrangement to provide needed supports and services to college students with Asperger syndrome.

Duffy, K. & Grandin, T. (2004). *Developing talents: Careers for individuals with Asperger syndrome and high-functioning autism.* Shawnee Mission, KS: Autism Asperger Publishing Co.

This career planning guide is written specifically for high-functioning adolescents and young adults on the autism spectrum, their families, teachers, and counselors. The two authors weave together a unique blend of information and advice based on personal experiences. Temple Grandin draws from her own experience with autism spectrum disorders and her professional career, and Kate Duffy uses her expertise on employment issues and experience as the mother of two teenagers with autistic-like behaviors. The result is an extremely useful and practical book that introduces step-by-step processes for the job search with a major section on the impact ASD has in the workplace, including managing sensory problems, how to nurture and turn talents and special interests into paid work, jobs that are particularly suited to individuals on the spectrum, and much more.

Fitzgerald, M., Harpur, J., & Lawlor, M. (2004) *Succeeding in college with Asperger syndrome: A student guide.* London: Jessica Kingsley Publishers.

College life is particularly stressful for students with Asperger syndrome and the resources that colleges provide for such students are often inadequate. This handbook provides information to help these students prepare for college-level studying, interact with staff and fellow students, cope with expectations and pressure, and understand their academic and domestic responsibilities. Drawing on first-hand interviews with students who have Asperger syndrome as well as direct clinical experience, the authors address these and many other questions, and make practical recommendations. This book is also valuable for educators as it provides key insights into the behavior and challenges of students with Asperger syndrome.

Freedman, S. (2010). *Developing college skills in students with autism and Asperger's syndrome*. London: Jessica Kingsley Publishers.

Going to college can be a daunting prospect for any young person, but for teenagers on the autism spectrum this is especially true. *Developing College Skills in Students with Autism and Asperger's Syndrome* describes the unique needs that ASD students entering further or higher education are likely to have. This book identifies several necessary skill sets, along with effective intervention strategies for facilitating skill development throughout the student's elementary, middle, and high school years. Several specific accommodations, supports, and classroom/teaching strategies that benefit students with ASD are presented. The book also provides ideas for any professional working with individuals on the autism spectrum, including mental health professionals, special educators, educational therapists, speech and language pathologists, occupational therapists, and high school and college counselors.

Grandin, T. (2006). *Thinking in pictures: My life with autism (expanded, tie-in edition)*. New York: Random House, Inc.

In this extraordinary book, Dr. Temple Grandin, a world renowned author, animal scientist, and autism advocate, writes from the dual perspectives of a scientist and an autistic person. She conveys to the reader how she managed to breach the boundaries of autism to function in the outside world.

Jamieson, C. & Jamieson J. (2004). *Managing Asperger syndrome at college and university*. London: David Fulton Publishers.

Meeting the demands of student life can be challenging, especially for students with Asperger syndrome. This book contains practical suggestions on how to make the postsecondary educational experience a good one. Advice is based upon sound knowledge of theory and practice and includes: taking steps towards selecting the right course at the right institution; coping strategies to use in academic and social situations; advice to help students who are living away from home; information on time-saving resources; how other students, tutors, and disability services can help; and useful references and addresses showing where to go next.

Karten, T. (2007). *More inclusion strategies that work! Aligning student strengths with standards*. Thousand Oaks, CA: Corwin Press.

This book provides research-based strategies for identifying and meeting the needs of students with disabilities, links best inclusive practices with content-specific curriculum, and helps educators fulfill IDEA 2004 requirements.

Martin, R. (2011). *Top tips for Asperger students: How to get the most out of university and college*. London: Jessica Kingsley Publishers.

Leaving home and moving to college or university can be a daunting experience. In this easy-to-use book, Rosemary Martin provides guidelines and advice for every student on the autism spectrum as he/she thinks about, and plans for, entry into college life. Containing effective methods for coping and succeeding away from home that cover every aspect of student life, this book focuses on the particular needs of people with autism and encourages everyone to make the most of student life in a style that suits them.

Myles, B. & Simpson, R. (2002). Asperger syndrome: An overview of characteristics. *Focus on Autism and Other Developmental Disabilities, 17*(3), 132–137.

Although the prevalence of Asperger syndrome is increasing, many children and youth who exhibit characteristics associated with this disability are not diagnosed until their later years. Because early intervention appears to be critical for individuals with Asperger syndrome, it is important that educators, families, and physicians have a comprehensive understanding of this complex exceptionality. This article, in an attempt to meet the aforementioned need, describes the characteristics of Asperger syndrome and its impact in the home, school, and community.

Palmer, A. (2006). *Realizing the college dream with autism or Asperger syndrome: A parent's guide to student success.* London: Jessica Kingsley Publishers.

This book is both a practical and a personal account of one ASD student's successful experience of going to college. It focuses on the entire postsecondary experience, from applying to making the most of the time once there. Ann Palmer advises parents and professionals on how to prepare the student for the transition from school and home life to a new environment and educational challenge, as well as how to support them through potential problems such as academic pressure, living away from home, social integration, and appropriate levels of participation in college.

Prince-Hughes, D. (2002). *Aquamarine blue 5: Personal stories of college students with autism.* Athens, OH: Ohio University Press.

The first book to be written by college students on the spectrum who have been diagnosed with Asperger's syndrome or high-functioning autism, *Aquamarine Blue 5* demonstrates their unique way of looking at and solving problems, and the challenges they face. These readable essays detail the struggles of a highly sensitive group and show that there are gifts specific to autistic students that enrich the university system, scholarship, and the world as a whole. Containing the stories of a dozen autistic students, this book deals with learning to eat in dormitory dining halls, managing classes, and making friends.

Sicile-Kira, C. (2004). *Autism spectrum disorders: The complete guide to understanding autism, Asperger's syndrome, pervasive developmental disorder, and other ASDs.* New York: Penguin Group Inc.

This books covers all aspects of autism conditions, including Asperger's syndrome and pervasive developmental disorder, including the following: the causes of autism spectrum disorders; how to properly diagnose ASDs; treatments based on physiology, sensory, and biomedical interventions; coping strategies for families; educational programs; living and working conditions for adults with ASD; and Autism Treatment Evaluation Checklist (ATEC).

Simpson C. & Spencer, V. (2009). *Success for students with learning disabilities: Strategies and tips to make the most of your college experience.* Waco, TX: Prufrock Press Inc.

Planning for college can be one of the most exciting times in a teen's life, but for those students with learning and other disabilities, the college experience can be fraught with frustration, uncertainty, and lowered self-confidence. *College Success for Students with Learning Disabilities* offers teens the confidence, strategies, and guidance they need to effectively choose a college, get prepared for university life, and make the most of their collegiate experience. The book covers pertinent topics such as understanding the rights and responsibilities of students with special needs, talking to professors and peers, getting involved, asking for and receiving accommodations, and utilizing one's strengths to meet and exceed academic standards. This unique reference book also includes advice from current college students with disabilities to empower future students and provide them with hope for success.

Vizard, D. (2009). *Meeting the needs of disaffected students: Engaging students with social, emotional and behavioral difficulties.* London: Continuum International Publishing Group.

Written for educators, this book offers a wide range of tried-and-tested activities to engage disaffected students and ensure that they have a successful learning experience. Through the use of a variety of approaches and techniques, including emotional literacy, neuro-linguistic programming, and learning styles, this resource gives practical examples of how to engage disaffected students and ensure they have a successful learning experience. The book outlines the causes of disaffection generally and looks at a range of syndromes and conditions that may give rise to disaffection, offering support strategies that will encourage the engagement of such students. Vizard also outlines approaches for helping students to self-manage their behavior and learning. *Meeting the Needs of Disaffected Students* is a wide-ranging and highly practical series which will help classroom practitioners to ensure that all students have a successful learning experience whatever their particular needs.

Universal Design for Learning and Disability-Friendly Environments

Web Resources

Center for Applied Special Technology (CAST)

What is Universal Design for Learning?

http:// www.cast.org/research/udl

CAST is a nonprofit research and development organization that works to expand learning opportunities for all individuals, especially those with disabilities, through Universal Design for Learning (UDL). Founded in 1984 as the Center for Applied

Special Technology, CAST has earned international recognition for its innovative contributions to educational products, classroom practices, strategies, and policies. Its staff includes specialists in education research and policy, neuropsychology, clinical/school psychology, technology, engineering, curriculum development, K-12 professional development, and more. This website explores the principles and applications of UDL and provides a comprehensive array of resources for educators.

DO-IT (Disabilities, Opportunities, Interworking, and Technology), University of Washington: AccessCollege: Systemic Change for Postsecondary Institutions

http://www.washington.edu/doit/Brochures/Academics/access_college.html

AccessCollege was developed by the University of Washington DO-IT (Disabilities, Opportunities, Internetworking, and Technology) office through a U.S. Department of Education Office of Postsecondary Education (OPE) funded grant, which created professional development materials and trained faculty and academic administrators nationwide to more fully include students with disabilities in their courses. This resource provides links to comprehensive websites designed for faculty, student services professionals, and administrators:

- **The Board Room**. A place for higher-level administrators at postsecondary institutions to learn about how to create and facilitate the development of courses and services that are accessible to all students, including those with disabilities.
- **The Center for Universal Design in Education**. A collection of web-based resources to help educators apply universal design to all aspects of the educational experience.

- **The Employment Office.** Information, resources, and promising practices for the purpose of increasing access to careers for individuals with disabilities.
- **The Student Services Conference Room.** A space for staff and administrators at postsecondary institutions to learn how to create facilities, services, and information resources that are accessible to all students, including those with disabilities. Within these websites are guidelines and information that lead to more accessible courses and programs and that help students with disabilities prepare for success in college.
- **The Faculty Room.** A space for faculty and administrators at postsecondary institutions to learn about how to create classroom environments and academic activities that maximize the learning of all students, including those with disabilities.

Much of the content is duplicated in other publications, training materials, and web pages also published by DO-IT. It includes six primary areas that address issues faced by postsecondary educators: accommodations and Universal Design; rights and responsibilities; faculty resources; faculty presentations; resources for trainers, staff, and administrators; and a searchable knowledge base.

DO-IT (Disabilities, Opportunities, Interworking, and Technology), University of Washington: Resources for Student Services Staff

http://www.washington.edu/doit/Conf/staff_resources.html

DO-IT offers a wide variety of publications and videos of particular interest to postsecondary student services administrators and staff working with students who have disabilities, including information on Universal Design for Learning, advising, tutoring, student development, residential life, career services, etc. Permission is granted to duplicate these materials in whole or in part as long as the source is acknowledged.

FAME (Faculty and Administrator Modules in Higher Education)

http://fame.oln.org/help_1.html

FAME is a website designed as a professional development tool for use in higher education. It contains information on how college faculty, administrators, disability service providers, and students can work individually and collaboratively to improve the accommodations, teaching–learning process, and overall campus environment for students with disabilities. Information on this website is divided into five discrete but interrelated modules:

- **Rights and responsibilities** of faculty, students, and disability service providers in the accommodations and instructional process
- **Universal Design for Learning** approach to instruction
- **Web accessibility** and assistive technology
- **College writing** challenges and effective teaching
- **Assessment of the campus climate** towards students with disabilities

National Center on Universal Design for Learning

www.udlcenter.org

Founded in 2009, the National UDL Center supports the effective implementation of UDL by connecting stakeholders in the field and providing comprehensive resources and information about UDL, advocacy, implementation, research, connections, and resources. There is a variety of materials on how to infuse UDL into curriculum and in the classroom.

Office of Special Education Programs (OSEP), U.S. Department of Education. OSEP: Ideas That Work

http://www.osepideasthatwork.org/udl/index.asp

This U.S. Department of Education site offers a comprehensive toolkit for teaching, engaging, and assessing students with disabilities. It contains information on, and links to, important resources, assistive technology, products, and instructional practices.

The Center for Universal Design in Education (CUDE), University of Washington

http://www.washington.edu/doit/CUDE

CUDE develops and collects web-based resources to help educators apply universal design to all aspects of the educational experience: instruction; student services, information technology, and physical spaces.

The Center for Universal Design, North Carolina State University

http://www.design.ncsu.edu/cud/about_ud/udprinciples.html

The Center for Universal Design, an initiative of the College of Design, is a national information, technical assistance, and research center that evaluates, develops, and promotes accessible and universal design in housing, commercial and public facilities, outdoor environments, and products. Its mission is to improve environments and products through design innovation, research, education and design assistance.

Books, Articles, and Online Brochures

Basham, J. D., Israel, I., Graden, K., Poth, R., & Winston, M. (2010). A comprehensive approach to RtI: Embedding universal design for learning and technology. *Learning Disability Quarterly, 33*(4), 243–255.

Response to Intervention (RtI) provides tiered levels of support to all students and allows for increasingly more intensive and individualized instruction. Similarly, Universal Design for Learning (UDL) addresses needs of students by proactively planning for instructional, environmental, and technology supports to allow all students to effectively access and engage in instruction. Although these two frameworks are widely accepted as structures for supporting students with diverse learning needs, the relationship between them has not been adequately developed. This article describes how an ecological RtI framework that integrates scientifically based instructional strategies, proactive instructional design, and purposeful technology use can provide a more seamless support system for all students.

Burgstahler, S. (2007). Universal design in education: Process, principles, and applications. Seattle: University of Washington. Retrieved from http://www.washington.edu/doit/Brochures/Programs/ud.html

This online brochure discusses the definition, principles, process, merits, and application of Universal Design in Education for a variety of settings, products, strategies, and environments. This includes classrooms, teaching methods, computer labs, services, physical spaces, etc. It also stresses that making a product or an environment accessible to people with disabilities often benefits others.

Burgstahler, S. E. (2007). Universal design of instruction: Definition, principles, guidelines, and examples. Seattle: University of Washington. Retrieved from http://www.washington.edu/doit/Brochures/Academics/instruction.html

This brochure was designed for educators to meet the needs of the ever-changing population of students in terms of their backgrounds, ages, learning styles, and abilities/disabilities. The definition, principles, and guidelines of *Universal Design of Instruction* are clearly outlined in this brochure. Additionally, it offers examples that educators can use to create courses that ensure lectures, discussions, visual aids, videos, printed materials, labs, and fieldwork are accessible to all students.

Burgstahler, S. E. & Cory, R. C. (Eds.) (2008). *Universal design in higher education: From principles to practice.* Cambridge, MA: Harvard Education Press.

A guide for researchers and practitioners, this book describes how to create fully accessible college and university programs. Topics include universal design of instruction, assessments, student services, physical environments, and technological environments. The comprehensive text examines how to institutionalize universal design in higher education settings.

Burgstahler, S., & Moore, E. (2009). Making student services welcoming and accessible through accommodations and universal design. *Journal of Postsecondary Education & Disability, 21*(3), 155–174.

This exploratory study focuses on the experience of students with disabilities and practitioners who identified access problems encountered in postsecondary education as well as potential solutions to these problems. Recommendations include increased staff/educator knowledge regarding disabilities (especially "invisible" disabilities that are not disclosed by service users); communication and accommodation strategies; rights and responsibilities; campus resources; and issues unique to specific offices. The authors share general approaches, categorized as the delivery of accommodations and the application of universal design, and specific onsite and online training materials that address issues identified in this study.

Center for Applied Special Technology. (2011). *Universal design for learning guidelines.* (Version 2.0). Wakefield, MA: Center for Applied Special Technology. Retrieved from http://www.udlcenter.org/aboutudl/udl guidelines

Universal Design for Learning Guidelines, an articulation of the UDL framework, was created to assist educators in planning lessons/units of study or developing curriculum (goals, methods, materials, and assessments) to reduce barriers, as well as optimize levels of challenge and support, to meet the needs of all learners from the start. They can also help educators identify the barriers found in existing curriculum. The UDL guidelines are organized according to the three main principles of UDL that address representation, expression, and engagement. For each of these areas, specific "checkpoints" for options are highlighted, followed by examples of practical suggestions.

Council for Exceptional Children. (2005). *Universal Design for Learning: A guide for teachers and education professionals.* Arlington, VA: Pearson, Merrill Prentice Hall.

This practical guide shows teachers how to understand, plan, and implement Universal Design for Learning in the classroom as well as in other academic environments. Offering various instructional resources, this book explains the general principles of UDL and shows educators how to effectively instruct students utilizing this research-based concept across content areas.

Izzo, M. V., Murray, A., Novak, J. (2008). The faculty perspective on universal design for learning. *Journal of Postsecondary Education and Disability, 21*(2), 60–72.

This article presents the results of two studies on the applicability and use of universal design in higher education. A web-based, self-paced, multi-modal professional development tool called FAME (Faculty and Administrator Modules in Higher Education) was developed, piloted, and revised in response to the training needs identified in these studies. Implications and specific UDL guidelines for providing educational access to students with disabilities are discussed.

Kumar, K., (2010). A journey towards creating an inclusive classroom: How universal design for learning has transformed my teaching. *Transformative Dialogues: Teaching & Learning Journal, 4*(2). Retrieved from http://kwantlen.ca/TD/TD.4.2/TD.4.2.5_Kumar_Inclusive_Classroom.pdf

This article describes the author's journey towards creating an inclusive classroom. An overview of the path that led her towards Universal Design for Learning from teaching to her own learning style, to recognizing diversity in her learners, and to ultimately attempting to facilitate success of all students (including those with learning limitations such as learning disabilities) is described.

Leichliter, M. (2010). *A case study of universal design for learning applied in the college classroom.* (Doctoral dissertation). Retrieved from ProQuest Dissertations & Theses. (AAT 3420378)

As the landscape of education and the demographics of the postsecondary classroom continue to evolve, so too must the teaching practices at our nation's institutions of higher education. This study follows an instructor who has evolved to incorporate Universal Design for Learning techniques into her classroom. This qualitative, descriptive case study addresses how and to what extent UDL techniques were implemented in the college classroom as well as the students' perceptions of them. Results indicated that the majority of students both acknowledged and positively received these techniques.

Meo, G. (2008). Curriculum planning for all learners: Applying universal design for learning (UDL) to a high school reading comprehension program. *Preventing School Failure, 52*(2), 21–30.

The Universal Design for Learning principles provide a blueprint for designing a curriculum that addresses the diverse needs of all learners. The author provides an overview of UDL, connections to curriculum planning, and practical techniques that guide general and special education teachers in planning and implementing curriculum, using the planning for all learners (PAL) procedures. PAL is a four-step process for designing and implementing a curriculum (goals, methods, materials, and assessments) that is accessible and effective for all learners. In this article, the author focuses on high school social studies content with a goal of supporting all students' understanding of the content by bringing together principles of UDL, the PAL process, and research-based reading comprehension strategies.

Michael, M. G. & Trezek, B. J. (2006). Universal design and multiple literacies: Creating access and ownership for students with disabilities. *Theory into Practice, 45*(4), 311–318.

Given the prevalence of reading and writing difficulties among students with disabilities, coupled with the high number of these students accessing the general education curriculum and instruction for the majority of their school day, providing access to general education curriculum and grade level academic content is a challenging task for general and special education teachers alike. In this article, the authors explore the concept of universal design and multiple literacies as a means of not only providing equal access to general education curriculum and instructional goals, but also providing opportunity for the development of literate thought for all students. They explore the use of both technological- and nontechnological-based strategies and methods of instruction and discuss the impact of using universal design as a means of providing educational justice for all students.

National Education Association. (2008). *Universal design for learning (UDL): Making learning accessible and engaging for all students.* (NEA Policy Brief, PB23). Washington, DC: NEA Education Policy and Practice Department. Retrieved from http://www.nea.org/assets/docs/PB_UDL. pdf
This policy brief provides the definition and basic principles of UDL as well as its use in the general curriculum; exemplary models around the nation; and strategies and technologies that can bridge the gap in learner skills, interests, and needs.

Ouellett, M. L. (2004). Faculty development and universal instructional design. *Equity & Excellence in Education, 37*, 135–144.
Centers for teaching and instructional development offer consultation services and resources materials for faculty members and graduate teaching assistants designed to promote excellence in undergraduate teaching. This article considers how such efforts may better address the needs of students with disabilities enrolled in postsecondary education by exploring the intersections of instructional development models.

Rose, D. & Meyer, A. (2002). *Teaching every student in the digital age: Universal design for learning.* Alexandria, VA: Association for Supervision and Curriculum Development.
This book is the first comprehensive presentation of the principles and applications of Universal Design for Learning—a practical, research-based framework for responding to individual learning differences and a blueprint for the modern redesign of education. Along with references to digital tools and links to online resources, the authors provide a set of templates to facilitate classroom implementation of UDL, share the experience of

a school district already succeeding with UDL, and highlight plans for UDL implementation on a national scale.

Schelly, C. L., Davies, P. L., & Spooner, C. L. (2011). Student perceptions of faculty implementation of universal design for learning. *Journal of Postsecondary Education and Disability, 24*(1), 17–28. Retrieved from http://accessproject.colostate.edu/assets/PDFs/Schelly,%20Davies,%20Spooner%202011.pdf

The anecdotal benefits of implementing Universal Design for Learning at postsecondary institutions are well documented. The literature suggests that UDL offers students with disabilities enhanced opportunities for engagement, expression, and academic performance. Responding to the call by educators for empirical evidence of UDL's beneficial effects on student learning, performance, persistence, and ultimately retention, this study measured changes and/or improvements in instruction as perceived by students following UDL instructor training and subsequent course delivery modifications. This study also describes the process that was undertaken to develop and implement pre- and post-student surveys, and points the way toward further research regarding the benefits of UDL implementation to postsecondary education.

Smith, F. G. (2008). *Perceptions of universal design for learning (UDL) in college classrooms.* (Doctoral dissertation). Retrieved from ProQuest Dissertations & Theses. (AAT 3296852)

The purpose of this mixed-methods study was to determine the relationship between the use of Universal Design for Learning strategies and the level of student interest and engagement in college classrooms at a public university and a private university in the United States. Student and faculty perceptions were examined. The study demonstrates a clear and positive relationship between student interest and engagement when UDL strategies were applied.

Sopko, V. (2009). *Universal design for learning: Policy challenges and recommendations*. Alexandria, VA: Project Forum at National Association of State Directors of Education.

This policy forum proceedings document from Project Forum of the National Association of State Directors of Special Education (NASDSE) includes federal education regulatory language for Universal Design for Learning. It summarizes panel presentations from the higher education perspective at the local, state, and national level. It also includes suggestions and proposed strategies to improve policy to impact implementation of UDL discussed throughout the panel and during the subsequent group discussions.

Spooner, F., Baker, J. N., Harris, A. A., Ahlgrim-Delzell, L., & Browder, D. (2007). Effects of training in universal design for learning (UDL) on lesson plan development. *Remedial and Special Education, 23*, 108–116.

This study investigated the effects of training in Universal Design for Learning on lesson plan development of special and general educators in a college classroom environment. The results suggest that a simple introduction to UDL can help educators design a lesson plan accessible for all students.

Wyndham, S. (2010). *School faculty perceptions of the use of technology to accommodate diverse learners: A universal design for learning framework*. (Doctoral dissertation). Retrieved from ProQuest Dissertations & Theses. (AAT 3426316)

The purpose of this study was to analyze how UDL training impacted school personnel's perceptions of inclusion, instruction, student engagement, and the use of technology to differentiate instruction to meet the needs of diverse learners. Significant differences were found in the perceptions that the primary responsibility for accommodating classroom activities for students with disabilities lies with the special education teacher as well as whether accommodations designed for students with disabilities create increased opportunities for all learners. Significant differences were also found in how technology was used to provide choice and flexibility to students and differentiate instruction.

School-based Professional Development Resources for Faculty

Colorado State University

Colorado State University provides a web page that describes in detail the purpose of Universal Design for Learning: http://accessproject.colostate.edu/udl/documents/philosophy.cfm

The institution's website also supplies information to faculty members on the definitions of different disabilities and the strategies that professors can use to guide and effectively teach and communicate with these students. Additionally, the website informs students of the strategies they can undertake to achieve success in the classroom. An example of a faculty training module for autism can be found at: http://accessproject.colostate.edu/disability/modules/ASD/mod_ASD.cfm?display=pg_1

San Diego State University

Project Higher Ed was designed to enhance disability education and training for faculty and administrators in institutions of higher education. Specifically, the training is intended to build on their knowledge of disability as well as skills and strategies necessary for meeting the postsecondary needs of students with disabilities. The training modules are approximately 45 minutes in length, are organized by topic, and are self paced. In some cases there are online discussion opportunities with colleagues and other professionals: http://interwork.sdsu.edu/arpe/web_programs/higher_ed.html

Ohio State University

Ohio State University has on its website an instructor hand-book on how to teach students with disabilities. The handbook defines and addresses the types of disabilities that students may have, and the services and accommodations that the school makes available to them. The information guide also defines and promotes the idea of Universal Design for Learning: www. ods.ohio-state.edu/faculty/instructor-handbook-teaching-students-with-disabilities/

Sonoma State University

Sonoma State University's website offers faculty teaching/ engagement strategies that are useful for all students, especially those with disabilities: http://www.sonoma.edu/dss/Teach_ suggestions.shtml#adhd

University of Arkansas at Little Rock

This institution has a variety of training videos that educate faculty members on how to work with students who have various disabilities. For example, one video, "Make a Difference: Tips for Teaching Students Who Have Learning Disabilities," is 34 minutes long and provides accommodation strategies for working with students who have learning disabilities in the postsecondary education setting. The link to the list of videos is: http://ualr.edu/pace/index.php/home/products/

In addition, the website provides the following links:

- A description of Universal Design and the principles that guide this framework: http://ualr.edu/pace/index.php/ home/hot-topics/ud/

- Instruction on the 10 steps for Universal Design of Online Courses that are disability-friendly: http://ualr.edu/pace/tenstepsud/index.htm
- Resources that discuss and explain such issues as disability law, ADD, and psychiatric disabilities: http://ualr.edu/pace/index.php/home/resources/

University of Connecticut Center on Postsecondary Education and Disability

The Center on Postsecondary Education and Disability (CPED) has been a national leader in promoting access to postsecondary education for students with disabilities. Its work combines research-based evidence and professional training to inform the field and advance postsecondary education opportunities for students. This is accomplished through graduate coursework, our annual Postsecondary Disability Training Institute, research and model demonstration projects, conference presentations, and involvement and leadership in various professional, state, and national organizations. Additionally, the center offers resources on Universal Design for Instruction for traditional, online, and blended courses: http://www.cped.uconn.edu/UDI.html

University of Rochester

University of Rochester provides information on the types of disabilities that students may have and the strategies faculty can use to assist these students. Topics include: Disabling Myths; Responsibilities; Teaching Students With Disabilities; Teaching Strategies for Students With Learning Disabilities; Teaching Students With Visual Impairments; Teaching Students With

Physical Disabilities or With Hand-Function Limitations; Teaching Students Who are Deaf or Hard of Hearing; Teaching Students With a Psychological Impairment; Teaching Students With Speech Impairments; and Resources. The website can be found at: http://www.rochester.edu/ada/guide.html

Comorbidity and Autism (Anxiety and Depression)

Cavalier, J. (2009, January 19). Autistic depression. *Depression and Anxiety*. Retrieved from http://anxiety-self-help.net/depression-and-anxiety/autistic-depression-2/

This article discusses the possible causes of anxiety and depression in individuals with autism and ways to treat such feelings. Many tasks can make people with autism very anxious, especially if the task breaks usual routine because any change in routine can cause great anxiety. Cavalier discusses a number of traditional and nontraditional treatments that can be successfully used to treat such anxiety.

Ghaziuddin, M., Ghaziuddin, N., & Greden, J. (2002). Depression in persons with autism: Implications for research and clinical care. *Journal of Autism & Developmental Disorders, 32*(4), 299–306.

Although several studies have investigated the occurrence of medical and neurological conditions in persons with autism, relatively few reports have focused on the phenomenology and treatment of psychiatric disorders in this population. There is emerging evidence that depression is probably the most common psychiatric disorder that occurs in persons with autism. In this review, the authors examine a variety of factors that influence the presence of depression in this population. They also discuss the various forms of treatment available and highlight the need for early detection.

Livestrong Foundation. (n.d.). *Anxiety treatments for autism*. Retrieved from
http://www.livestrong.com/article/85613-anxiety-treatments-autism/
This article highlights a variety of medical, therapeutic, and alternative treatments for people with autism who also suffer from anxiety, depression, or obsessive-compulsive disorder (OCD).

Mazurek, M. O. & Kanne, S. M. (2010). Friendship and internalizing symptoms among children and adolescents with ASD. *Journal of Autism and Developmental Disabilities*, 40(12), 1512–1520.
Anxiety and depression are common among children and adolescents with autism spectrum disorders, highlighting a need to identify factors that protect against these symptoms. Among typically developing children, friendships are protective, and lead to better emotional outcomes. The current study examined a large, well-characterized sample of children and adolescents with ASD to examine the relations among friendship, ASD symptom severity, and anxiety/depression. Rates of anxiety/depression were high in this sample. Greater ASD severity was associated with fewer symptoms of anxiety/depression, lower IQ, and poorer number and/or quality of reciprocal friendships. Surprisingly, children with no or very poor dyadic relationships experienced less anxiety than those with existing, but limited, friendships. Implications and directions for future research are discussed.

National Autistic Society. (n.d.). Anxiety in adults with an autism spectrum disorder. Retrieved from http://www.autism.org.uk/living-with-autism/understanding-behaviour/anxiety-in-adults-with-an-autism-spectrum-disorder.aspx
The National Autistic Society, based in England, has a website that educates people about autism. In particular, the organization has a guide that informs people of how they can help individuals with autism manage their anxiety.

Self-determination

Abery, B. & Stancliffe, R. (1996). The ecology of self-determination. In D. J. Sands & M. L. Wehmeyer (Eds.), *Self-determination across the life span: Independence and choice for people with disabilities* (pp. 111–146). Baltimore: Paul H. Brookes.

This chapter explores the self-determination process from an ecological perspective—a framework that recognizes the contributions of the individual and the environment and the synergistic relationship that exists between the two. First, an argument is made for the necessity of taking an ecological approach to understanding self-determination. Second, an ecological framework for self-determination is presented, and the manner in which ecological factors influence both opportunities for personal control and the acquisition of the capacities necessary for self-determination is explored. Third, the implications of current work on the ecological antecedents of self-determination, for research, theory, and practice are discussed.

Ankeny, E. M. & Lehmann, J. P. (2011). Journey toward self-determination: Voices of students with disabilities who participated in a secondary transition program on a community college campus. *Remedial and Special Education, 32*(4), 279–289.

Four students with disabilities enrolled in a secondary transition program at a community college were interviewed to learn more about their transition experiences. One of the issues they touched on was self-determination. This study is a part of the larger qualitative narrative effort but with a specific focus on exploring participants' perceptions regarding their journey toward self-determination. Field and Hoffman's model of self-determination (i.e., know yourself, value yourself, plan, act and experience outcomes, and learn) guided the data re-examination. Themes found in students' stories were (a) personal factors associated with the construct of self-determination,

(b) environments and experiences that foster self-determination, and (c) the individualized education program meeting as a significant tool for supporting students' building of skills leading to self-determination. The journey toward self-determination for the four narrators was formative and complex and highlights the need to promote its practice. The authors conclude that the study's methodology promoting joint recollection and reflection about significant life events can enhance students' understanding and appreciation of their acquisition of self-determination skills.

Algozzine, B., Browder, D., Karvonen, M., Test, D. W., & Wood, W. M. (2001). Effects of interventions to promote self-determination for individuals with disabilities. *Review of Educational Research, 71*(2), 219–277.

Self-determination, the combination of skills, knowledge, and beliefs that enable a person to engage in goal-directed, self-regulated, autonomous behavior, has become an important part of special education and related services for people with disabilities. Research on the outcomes of self-determination interventions has been sparse. In this study, the authors conducted a comprehensive review of literature and used quantitative methods of meta-analysis to investigate: what self-determination interventions have been studied, what groups of individuals with disabilities have been taught self-determination, and what levels of outcomes have been achieved using self-determination interventions. The results demonstrate that self-determination can be taught and learned, and can make a difference in the lives of individuals with disabilities.

Bremer, C. D., Kachgal, M., & Schoeller, K. (2003). Self-determination: Supporting successful transition. *Research to Practice Brief: Improving Secondary Education and Transition Services through Research, 2*(1). Retrieved from http://www.ncset.org/publications/viewdesc.asp?id=962

This article discusses the principles behind self-determination and its importance in the education of students with disabilities.

The authors discuss how educators can create and maintain an environment conducive to self-determination, which can result in a measurable increase in self-sufficiency and an even greater sense of purpose and satisfaction in adulthood. Some of the tips described in this article to help develop self-determination skills include: promoting choice making, encouraging exploration of possibilities, advocating reasonable risk taking, encouraging problem solving, promoting self-advocacy, facilitating development of self-esteem, developing goal setting and planning, and helping youth understand their disabilities.

Field, S., Sarver, M. D., & Shaw, S. E (2003). Self-determination: A key to success in postsecondary education for students with learning disabilities. *Remedial and Special Education, 24,* 339–349.

This article provides a summary of research showing that grade point averages of postsecondary students with learning disabilities are correlated with perceived levels of self-determination. It is followed by discussion of characteristics of postsecondary environments that support self-determination, such as self-determined role models, self-determination skill instruction, opportunities for choice, positive communication patterns and relationships, availability of supports, and universal design for instruction.

Getzel, E. E. & Thoma, C. A. (2006). Voice of experience: What college students with learning disabilities and attention deficit/hyperactivity disorders tell us are important self-determination skills for success. *Learning Disabilities: A Multidisciplinary Journal, 14,* 33–39.

This article describes the results of a series of focus group interviews conducted with postsecondary students with disabilities about the importance of self-determination in their success in those settings. Approximately 40% of the student participants identified a learning disability or attention deficit disorder as their primary disability. The results discussed in the article are the thoughts and comments of these college students that were extracted from the focus group results, which indicated that self-determination skills were important to their success in taking courses, finding the supports they needed, and advocating for their rights. Implications for supports for students with disabilities in postsecondary settings are discussed.

Getzel, E. & Thoma, C. (2008). Experiences of college students with disabilities and the importance of self-determination in higher education settings. *Career Development for Exceptional Individuals, 31*(2), 77–84. Retrieved from ProQuest Psychology Journals. doi: 1536976131

Although the literature is clear that self-determination is an important component of the transition planning process for students with disabilities preparing for postsecondary education, further studies are needed to explore what self-determination strategies these students use to remain in college and successfully meet the challenges in postsecondary education settings. This article describes a study conducted with post-secondary education students in two- and four-year college settings to (a) identify skills that effective self-advocates use to ensure they stay in college and obtain needed supports, and (b) identify the essential self-determination skills needed to remain and persist in college. Findings from the study and implications for postsecondary education and secondary education are discussed.

Hoffman, A. (2003, August). Teaching decision making to students with learning disabilities by promoting self-determination. *ERIC EC Digest #E647*. Retrieved from http://www.tourettesyndrome.net/wp-content/uploads/Hoffman.pdf

The ability to make effective choices and decisions is one of the most important competencies students, including those with learning disabilities, need to be successful in life after high school. Promoting student self-determination provides an excellent framework within which to teach students how to make effective choices and decisions. Effective choices are those that the student will see as beneficial, and these models of self-determination can be used to teach students to make choices and decisions that: (a) are consistent with what is most important to them, and (b) enable them to achieve more positive adult outcomes. This digest specifically examines how instructional practices to promote self-determination can be used to help students with learning disabilities make effective choices and decisions.

Kaff, M. (2009, March 29). *Making the grade: What advisors and administrators need to know to better assist students with disabilities* [Webinar Handout]. Retrieved from http://www.nacada.ksu.edu/Webinars/documents/W24HandoutforParticipants_000.pdf

This webinar handout contains a helpful grid on characteristics and practices that support the development of self-determination.

Mithaug, D., Wehmeyer, M., Agran, M., Martin, J., & Palmer, S. (1998). In M. L. Wehmeyer & D. J. Sands (Eds.), *Making it happen: Student involvement in education planning, decision making and instruction* (pp. 299–328). Baltimore: Paul H. Brookes.

Teachers seeking to promote the self-determination of their students must enable them to become self-regulated problem-solvers. This chapter introduces a model of teaching, The Self-Determined Learning Model of Instruction, incorporating principles of self-determination, which enables educators to teach students to become causal agents in their own lives. This model was field-tested with students with disabilities. Students receiving instruction from teachers using the model attained educationally relevant goals, showed enhanced self-determination, and communicated their satisfaction with the process. Teachers implementing the model likewise indicated their satisfaction with the process and suggested that they would continue to use the model after the completion of the field test.

NCSET. (n.d.). Self-determination for postsecondary students. Retrieved from http://www.ncset.org/topics/sdpse/default.asp?topic=7

Postsecondary education and training is considered a gateway to high-skilled jobs of the 21st Century. Although more students with disabilities are entering higher education than in the past, the majority leave before completing their program or degree. One reason is that many youth with disabilities lack the self-determination skills—such as the ability to articulate their strengths and advocate for their needs—necessary for success in postsecondary education programs and ultimately the workplace. Without necessary accommodations, students with disabilities may become discouraged with their lack of success and may discontinue their postsecondary education. A possible explanation for students' limited development of self-determination is that many educators are unaware of how to help them develop such skills. In addition, students may have limited opportunities to make choices and act independently. As a result, many students with disabilities exit high school with little experience in self-advocacy, which is an important self-determination skill for negotiating new responsibilities in postsecondary education and the workplace.

This website explores how self-determination—the combined skills of self-awareness, self-advocacy, self-efficacy, decision-making, independent performance, self-evaluation, and adjustment—can contribute to an individual's ability to establish and achieve his/her own goals during and after higher education experiences. It includes frequently asked questions, related research, emerging and promising practices, websites, and additional resources.

Shogren, K. A. (2011). Culture and self-determination: A synthesis of the literature and directions for future research and practice. *Career Development for Exceptional Individuals, 34*(2), 115–127.

Self-determination has received significant attention in the special education field, but scholars' knowledge of how culturally and linguistically diverse learners and their families perceive interventions to promote self-determination remains limited. Understanding how the construct is perceived in diverse cultures is critically important given the growing diversity of society. This article reviewed existing research and scholarship examining the relation between culture and self-determination in students with disabilities. In all, 10 theoretical, review, and research articles that specifically addressed this topic were identified. Generally, the body of scholarship suggests that the self-determination construct could have universal value if a flexible framework that considers cultural and systems-level variables is utilized to develop individualized interventions. Implications for future research and practice are discussed.

University of Illinois at Chicago National Research & Training Center. (2002). *Self-determination framework for people with psychiatric disabilities.* Retrieved from http://www.psych.uic.edu/UICNRTC/sdframe work.pdf

This article explains and describes the three levels of self-determination. The first level is individual or internal self-determination/recovery. This level highlights the importance of individual empowerment to fulfill one's own capacity for self-determination and recovery. The second level is mental health services, supports, and policies that foster self-determination. This level pertains to public and private service systems, as well as among informal caregivers and peers, that foster self-determination. The third level is collective, social, or shared self-determination. This level focuses on the social, cultural, political, and economic context in which people live, vote, work, and participate in community activities, raise families, socialize, and otherwise relate to each other casually or intimately, individually or in groups.

Wehmeyer, M. (2002). Self-determination and the education of students with disabilities. *ERIC EC Digest #E632*. Arlington, VA: ERIC Clearinghouse on Disabilities and Gifted Education.

Promoting self-determination has been recognized as best practice in the education of adolescents with disabilities since the early 1990s, when the Individuals with Disabilities Education Act (IDEA) mandated increased student involvement in transition planning. Promoting self-determination involves addressing the knowledge, skills, and attitudes students will need to take more control over and responsibility for their lives. Students with disabilities who are self-determined are more likely to succeed as adults, and efforts to build self-determination skills are integrated into the practices of schools that provide high-quality transition programs. However, promoting self-determination should not begin in high school. Students in elementary and middle school need to receive such instruction as well.

Wehmeyer, M. L. (2007). Promoting self-determination in students with developmental disabilities. New York: Guildford Press.

Based on empirical research, this book offers comprehensive information on how to promote self-determination in students with disabilities. Specifically, it provides proven, practical strategies for classroom instruction.

Wehmeyer, M. L., Kelchner, K., & Richards, S. (1996). Essential characteristics of self-determined behavior in individuals with mental retardation. *American Journal on Mental Retardation, 100*(6), 632–642.

Despite increased emphasis on self-determination for individuals with mental retardation, only a few theoretical models have been formulated that specify measurable characteristics for the promotion and evaluation of this outcome. The authors propose that self-determination refers to acting as the primary causal agent in one's life and making choices and decisions regarding one's quality of life free from undue external influence or interference. Self-determined behavior is autonomous, self-regulated, based on psychological empowerment, and self-realizing. The authors evaluated this definition by asking participants with mental retardation to complete various instruments that measured self-determined behavior and these essential characteristics. Discriminant function analysis indicated that measures of essential characteristics predicted differences between groups based on exhibition of self-determined behavior.

Wehmeyer, M. & Schwartz, M. (1997). Self-determination and positive adult outcomes: A follow-up study of youth with mental retardation or learning disabilities. *Exceptional Children*, *63*(2), 245–255.

There is increased emphasis on self-determination as an important outcome for youth with disabilities if they are to achieve positive adult outcomes after they leave school. However, the causal link between self-determination and positive adult outcomes has remained untested. The outcomes of the study outlined in this article revealed that self-determined students with disabilities were more likely to have achieved more positive adult outcomes, including being employed at a higher rate and earning more per hour, than peers who were not self-determined. A framework for promoting self-determination as an educational outcome is presented.

Zager, D., Wehmeyer, M. L., & Simpson, R. L. (Eds.) (2012). *Educating students with autism spectrum disorders: Research-based principles and practices*. New York: Routledge.

Similar to a handbook in its comprehensive description of the theory and research supporting current practices in the treatment of autism spectrum disorders, this interdisciplinary text shows how the existing knowledge base can be used to explore promising new possibilities related to the field's many unanswered questions.

APPENDIX A

Survey of Faculty Experiences with ASD in College Classrooms

In the next decade an increasing number of students with behavior and learning challenges will be entering your classes. Many of you have already taught students with disabilities who receive various kinds of accommodations. The Pace Center has received a grant from Autism Speaks to help faculty prepare for these students, especially those on the autism spectrum. Your responses to the following questions will help guide the development of faculty support materials. Please feel free to add your comments.

I HAVE OBSERVED THE FOLLOWING BEHAVIORS:

1. Difficulty learning from lecture format

	No. of respondents	Response %
Frequently	13	10.7
Occasionally	68	56.2
Never	11	9.1
Not applicable	29	24.0
Total	121	100

2. Difficulty answering questions in class

	Response %	No. of respondents
Frequently	21.7	15
Occasionally	58.0	40
Never	14.5	10
Not Applicable	5.8	4
Total	*100*	*69*

3. Difficulty asking questions in class

	Response %	No. of respondents
Frequently	20.3	14
Occasionally	55.1	38
Never	18.8	13
Not Applicable	5.8	4
Total	*100*	*69*

4. Limited comprehension of abstract/complex nuanced information

	Response %	No. of respondents
Frequently	29.0	20
Occasionally	58.0	40
Never	4.3	3
Not Applicable	8.7	6
Total	*100*	*69*

5. Home assignments do not reflect in class learning

	Response %	No. of respondents
Frequently	11.6	8
Occasionally	49.3	34
Never	15.9	11
Not Applicable	23.2	16
Total	*100*	*69*

6. Difficulty working in groups

	Response %	No. of respondents
Frequently	18.85	13
Occasionally	46.40	32
Never	13.00	9
Not Applicable	21.75	15
Total	*100*	*69*

7. Difficulty understanding alternative points of view

	Response %	No. of respondents
Frequently	17.4	12
Occasionally	50.7	35
Never	17.4	12
Not Applicable	14.5	10
Total	*100*	*69*

8. Going off topic in discussions

	Response %	No. of respondents
Frequently	29.0	20
Occasionally	43.5	30
Never	14.5	10
Not Applicable	13.0	9
Total	*100*	*69*

9. Monopolizing class discussion

	Response %	No. of respondents
Frequently	14.50	10
Occasionally	53.60	37
Never	21.75	15
Not Applicable	10.15	7
Total	*100*	*69*

10. Lack of impulse control, e.g. calling out in class, leaving the room suddenly

	Response %	No. of respondents
Frequently	20.3	14
Occasionally	37.7	26
Never	29.0	20
Not Applicable	13.0	9
Total	*100*	*69*

11. Unusual nonverbal behaviors, e.g. eye contact, fidgeting, posture

	Response %	No. of respondents
Frequently	20.30	14
Occasionally	50.70	35
Never	18.85	13
Not Applicable	10.15	7
Total	100	69

12. Distractibility

	Response %	No. of respondents
Frequently	29.0	18
Occasionally	56.5	35
Never	6.4	4
Not Applicable	8.1	5
Total	100	62

13. Chronic lateness or absence

	Response %	No. of respondents
Frequently	18.8	13
Occasionally	46.4	32
Never	29.0	20
Not Applicable	5.8	4
Total	100	69

14. Disorganization and/or poor time management

	Response %	No. of respondents
Frequently	29.00	20
Occasionally	50.70	35
Never	10.15	7
Not Applicable	10.15	7
Total	*100*	*69*

15. Disrespectful language or behavior

	Response %	No. of respondents
Frequently	2.9	2
Occasionally	39.1	27
Never	52.2	36
Not Applicable	5.8	4
Total	*100*	*69*

16. Insensitive language or behavior

	Response %	No. of respondents
Frequently	2.90	2
Occasionally	44.93	31
Never	46.38	32
Not Applicable	5.79	4
Total	*100*	*69*

I HAVE PROVIDED THE FOLLOWING SUPPORT TO STUDENTS WITH THESE BEHAVIORS:

17. Adapting instructional style and class activities

	No. of respondents	Response %
Yes	32	51.6
No	30	48.4
Total	62	100

18. Providing support for long-term assignments

	Response %	No. of respondents
YES	65.6	42
NO	34.4	22
Total	100	64

19. Allowing rewrites, first drafts, etc.

	Response %	No. of respondents
YES	69.8	44
NO	30.2	19
Total	100	63

20. Extra opportunities for individual conferencing

	Response %	No. of respondents
YES	81.25	52
NO	18.75	12
Total	100	64

APPENDIX B

Universal Design for Learning Descriptors

The National Center on Universal Design for Learning (www. udlcenter.org) categorizes the **what, how,** and **why** of learning based on three different networks of the brain. The **what** of learning is related to the way in which facts are processed. The **how** of learning is related to the planning and organization of information, as discussed in the section on executive function in Chapter 2. The **why** of learning is related to the engagement and motivation for learning. Curriculum that is flexible offers multiple ways to present these aspects of learning.

Recognition Networks

The back of the brain regulates the five senses. This area allows us to identify sensory experiences. For example, if you were to hear a familiar tune your ability to identify it would come from this part of the brain. This is the **what** of learning: how we gather facts and categorize what we see, hear, and read.

Figure B.1
Recognition Networks

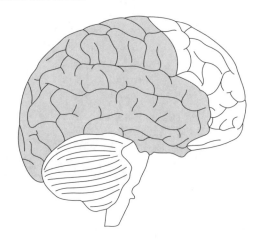

Strategic Networks

This area of the brain puts knowledge into action. The front of the brain is responsible for planning and initiating movement. If you were hitting a baseball you would engage the front part of the brain. This is the **how** of learning: how we plan and perform specific tasks, how we organize and express our ideas.

Figure B.2
Strategic Networks

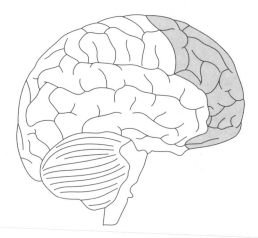

Affective Networks

This area of the brain is related to emotions and can impact motivation. It is designed to support evaluation of an activity or pattern. For example, if you have had a negative response to a certain type of food, this part of the brain will reduce your motivation to eat it again. This is the **why** of learning: how learners get engaged and stay motivated, how they are challenged, excited, or interested.

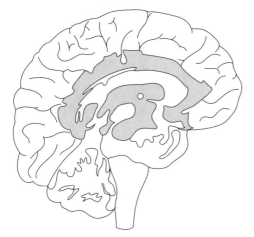

Figure B.3
Affective Networks

REFERENCES

Adams, C., Green, J., Gilchrist, A., & Cox, A. (2002). Conversational behavior of children with Asperger syndrome and conduct disorder. *Journal of Child Psychology and Psychiatry, 43,* 679–690.

Adreon, D., & Durocher, J. S. (2007). Evaluating the college transition needs of individuals with high-functioning autism spectrum disorders. *Intervention in School & Clinic, 42*(5), 271–279.

Alpern, C. & Zager, D. (2007). Addressing communication needs of young students with autism in a college-based inclusion program. *Education and Training in Developmental Disabilities, 42*(4), 428–436.

Anderson, D., Lord, C., Risi, S., Dilavore, P. S., Shulman, C., Thurm, A., et al. (2007). Patterns of growth in verbal abilities among children with autism spectrum disorder. *Journal of Counseling and Clinical Psychology, 75,* 594–604.

Azano, A. & Tuckwiller, E. D. (2011). GPS for the English classroom: Understanding executive dysfunction in secondary students, *Teaching Exceptional Children, 43,* 38–44.

Barbour, Q. (2008). ICI to enhance postsecondary education for individuals with developmental disabilities. Institute for Community Living. Retrieved from www.communityinclusion.org

Baron-Cohen, S., Leslie, A. M., Frith, U. (1985). Does the autistic child have a theory of mind? *Cognition, 21,* 37–46.

Bellon-Harn, M. L. & Harn, W. (2006). Profiles of social communicative competence in middle school children with Asperger syndrome: Two case studies. *Child Language Teaching and Therapy, 22,* 1–26.

Boyle, C. (2000, April). *Testimony on the Prevention of Developmental Disabilities,* U.S. Department of Health and Human Services. Washington, DC: House Committee on Government Reform.

Bregman, J. D. & Higdon, C. (2012). Definitions and clinical characteristics of autism spectrum disorders. In D. Zager, M. L. Wehmeyer, & R. L. Simpson (Eds.), *Educating students with autism spectrum disorders* (pp. 13–45). New York: Routledge.

Briel, L. W. & Getzel, E. E. (2005). Internships and field experiences. In E. E. Getzel & P. Wehman (Eds.), *Going to college: Expanding opportunities for people with disabilities,* (pp. 271–290). Baltimore: Paul H. Brookes.

Briel, L. W. & Wehman, P. (2005). Career planning and placement. In E. E. Getzel & P. Wehman (Eds.), *Going to college: Expanding opportunities for people with disabilities,* (pp. 291–306). Baltimore: Paul H. Brookes.

Brinton, B., Robinson, L. A., & Fujiki, M. (2004). Description of a program for social language intervention: "If you can have a conversation, you can have a relationship." *Language Speech and Hearing Services in the Schools, 35,* 283–290.

Camarena, P. M. & Sarigiani, P. A. (2009). Postsecondary educational aspirations of high-functioning adolescents with autism spectrum disorders and their parents. *Autism and Other Developmental Disabilities, 24*(2), 1–12.

Capps, L., Kehres, J., & Sigman, M. (1998). Conversational abilities among children with autism and children with developmental delays. *Autism, 2,* 325–344.

Charman, T., Baron-Cohen, S., Swettenham, J., Baird, G., Drew, A., & Cox, A. (2003). Predicting language outcome in infants with autism and pervasive developmental disorder. *International Journal of Language and Communication Disorders, 38*(3), 265–285.

Church, C., Alisanski, S., & Amanullah, S. (2000). The social, behavioral, and academic experiences of children with Asperger syndrome. *Focus on Autism and Other Developmental Disabilities, 15,* 12–20.

Clark, G. M. (2010). Foreword. In S. F. Shaw, J. W. Madaus, & L. L. Dukes, III (Eds.), *Preparing students with disabilities for college success: A practical guide to transition planning* (pp. xiii). Baltimore: Paul H. Brookes.

Dwyre, A., Grigal, M., & Fialka, J. (2010). Student and family perspectives. In M. Grigal & D. Hart (Eds.), *Think college: Postsecondary education options for students with intellectual disabilities* (pp. 189–227). Baltimore: Paul H. Brookes.

Eisenman, L. & Mancini, K. (2010). College perspectives and issues. In M. Grigal & D. Hart (Eds.), *Think college: Postsecondary education options for students with intellectual disabilities* (pp. 161–188). Baltimore: Paul H. Brookes.

Frith, U. (1989). Autism and theory of mind. In C. Gillberg (Ed.), *Diagnosis and treatment of autism* (pp. 33–52). New York: Plenum Press.

Grigal, M. & Hart, D. (2010). *Think college! Postsecondary education options for students with intellectual disabilities.* Baltimore: Paul. H. Brookes.

Howlin, P., Mawhood, L., & Rutter, N. (2000). Autism and developmental receptive language disorder—a follow-up comparison in early adult life. II: Social, behavioral, and psychiatric outcomes. *Journal of Child Psychology and Psychiatry, 41*(5), 561–578.

Hughes, C., Russell, J., & Robbins, T. W. (1994). Evidence for executive dysfunction in autism. *Neuropsychologia, 32*(4), 477–492.

Individuals with Disabilities Education Act of 2004, 20 U.S.C. § 1400 et seq. (2004).

Jesien, G. (2009, November). Postsecondary education for students with disabilities: Why and what can university centers for excellence in developmental disabilities contribute? Paper presented at the *NIDRR State of the Science Conference*, Fairfax, VA.

Klin, A., McPartland, J., & Volkmar, F. R. (2005). Asperger syndrome. In F. R. Volkmar, R. Paul, A. Klin, & D. Cohen (Eds.), *Handbook of autism and pervasive developmental disabilities* (3rd ed.) (pp. 88–125). Hoboken, NJ: John Wiley & Sons.

Kogan, M. D., Blumberg, S. J., Schieve, L. A., Boyle, C. A., Perrin, J. M., Ghandour, R. M., et al. (2009). Prevalence of parent-reported diagnosis of autism spectrum disorder among children in the US, 2007. *Pediatrics, 124*(5), 1395–1403.

McEvoy, R., Rogers, S. J., & Pennington, B. F. (1993). Executive function and social communication deficits in young autistic children. *Journal of Child Psychology and Psychiatry, 34*, 563–578.

Magliore, A., Butterworth, J., & Hart, D. (2009). Postsecondary education and employment outcomes for youth with intellectual disabilities. *Think College! Fast Facts,* 1. Retrieved from http://www.thinkcollegekansas.lsi.ku.edu/publications/FF_1.pdf

Miller, E. K. & Cohen, J. D. (2001) An integrative theory of prefrontal cortex function. *Annual Review of Neuroscience, 24*, 167–202.

Miller, E. K. & Wallis, J. D. (2009). Executive function and higher order cognition: Definition and neural substrates. In I. R. Squire (Ed.), *Encyclopedia of neuroscience* (Vol. 4, pp. 99–104). Oxford: Academic Press.

Miller, L. J. & Lane, S. J. (2000). Toward a consensus in terminology in sensory integration theory and practice. Part 1: Taxonomy of neurophysiological processes. *Sensory Integration Special Interest Section, 23*(1), 1–4.

New York State Education Department. (2009). *New York State annual performance report.* Albany, NY: University of the State of New York.

Ozonoff, S., Pennington, B. F., & Rogers, S. J. (1991). Executive function deficits in high-functioning autistic individuals: Relationship to theory of mind. *Journal of Child Psychology and Psychiatry, 32*(7), 1081–1105.

Paul, R., Orlovski, S. M., Marchinko, H. C., & Volkmer, R. (2009). Conversational behaviors in youth with high functioning ASD and Asperger syndrome. *Journal of Autism and Developmental Disorders, 39*,115–125.

Prizant, B. M., Wetherby, A. M., Rubin, E., & Laurent, A. C. (2003). The SCERTS model: A transactional, family centered approach to enhancing communication and socioemotional abilities of children with autism spectrum disorder. *Infants and Young Children, 16*(4), 296–316.

Rose, D. H., Harbour, W. S., Johnston, C. S., Daley, S. G., & Abarbanell, L. (2008). Universal design for learning in postsecondary education: Reflections on principles and their application. In S. E. Burgstahler & R. C. Cory (Eds.), *Universal design in higher education: From principles to practice* (pp. 3–20). Cambridge, MA: Harvard Education Press.

Rubin, E. & Lennon, L. (2004). Challenges in social communication in Asperger syndrome and high-functioning autism. *Topics in Language Disorders, 24*, 271–285.

Russell, J., Jarrold, C., & Hood, B. (1999). Two intact executive functions in autism: Implications for the nature of the disorder. *Journal of Autism and Developmental Disorders, 29*, 103–112.

Shriberg, L. D., Paul, R., McSweeny, J. L., Klin, A., Cohen, D. J., & Volkmar, F. R. (2001). Speech and prosody characteristics of adolescents and adults with high-functioning autism and Asperger syndrome. *Journal of Speech, Language and Hearing Research, 44*, 1097–1115.

Stodden, R. A., Yamamoto, K. K., & Folk, E. (2010). Preparing students with autism and intellectual disabilities for the postsecondary experience. *DADD Express, 21*(2), 1–6.

Toth, K., Munson, J., Meltzoff, A. N., & Dawson, G. (2006). Early predictors of communication development in young children with autism spectrum disorder: Joint attention, imitation, and toy play. *Journal of Autism and Developmental Disorders, 36*, 993–1005.

Tsatanis, K. D. (2005). Neuropsychological characteristics in autism and related conditions. In F. R. Volkmar, R. Paul, A. Klin, & D. Cohen (Eds.), *Handbook of autism and pervasive developmental disabilities* (3rd ed.) (pp. 365–381). Hoboken, NJ: John Wiley & Sons.

U.S. Department of Education. (2009, November). *State of the Science Conference on Postsecondary Education for Students with Intellectual Disabilities*, Fairfax, VA.

Weider, S. (2012). DIR—The developmental, individual difference, relationship-based model: A dynamic model for the 21st century. In D. Zager, M. L. Wehmeyer, & R. L. Simpson (Eds.), *Educating students with autism spectrum disorders: Research-based principles and practices* (pp. 82–98). New York: Routledge.

Wetherby, A. M., Prizant, B. M. & Schuler, A. L. (2000). Understanding the nature of communication and language impairments. In A. M. Wetherby & B. M. Prizant (Eds.), *Autism spectrum disorders: A transactional developmental perspective* (pp. 109–142). Baltimore: Paul H. Brookes.

White, S. W., Oswald, D., Ollendick, T., & Scahill, L. (2009). Anxiety in children with pervasive developmental disorders. *Clinical Psychology Review, 29,* 216–229.

Woods, J. J. & Wetherby, A. M. (2003). Early identification of and intervention for infants and toddlers who are at risk for autism spectrum disorder. *Language, Speech, and Hearing Services in the Schools, 34,* 180–193.

Yell, M. L., Ryan, J. B., Rozalski, M. E., & Katsiyannis, A. (2009). The U.S. Supreme Court and special education: 2005–2007. *Teaching Exceptional Children, 41*(3), 68–75.

Zager, D. & Alpern, C. (2010). College-based inclusion programming for transition-age students with autism. *Focus on Autism and Other Developmental Disabilities, 25,* 151–157.

INDEX

Note: 'F' after a page number indicates a figure; 't' indicates a table.

abstract concepts 10, 12, 22, 28, 33
accommodations 16–19, 35, 104t
affective networks 107f
Americans with Disabilities Act
    (1990) 5–6
anxiety 13–14, 27, 87–8
Asberger syndrome 65–70
assistive technology 19
Association on Higher Education
    and Disability (AHEAD) 59–60
attention deficit disorder (ADD) 15
auditory processing 29
Autism Research Institute (ARI) 60
Autism Society of America 60
Autism Speaks 61
Autism Spectrum Disorder (ASD):
    characteristics of students with
    7–15, 24–9; definition of 6–7;
    increasing rate of students with
    4–5. *See also* students with
    Autism Spectrum Disorder (ASD)

brain networks 106–7f

career planning 66
case studies 53–8

Center for Applied Special
    Technology (CAST) 71–2
Center for Autism and Related
    Disorders (CARD) 61
The Center for Universal Design,
    North Carolina State University 75
The Center for Universal Design in
    Education (CUDE), University of
    Washington 76
Centers for Disease Control (CDC)
    61
central coherence 32–4
classroom strategies: and
    assessments of student
    performance 43–4; for enhancing
    class participation 46–50;
    identifying "big picture" concepts
    33–4; and instructional pace 32;
    keeping discussions on-topic 47,
    55; for lecture-style classes 10, 12;
    and lesson structure 40; making
    information relevant 36;
    preparing students for class 38–9,
    42–3; presenting information in
    multiple formats 37; and "soft
    skills" 44–5; and user-friendly

design of materials 39–42; visual supports 37, 39–40, 65; written vs. oral instructions 31–2. *See also* case studies
college. *See* postsecondary education
Colorado State University 84
communication: and auditory processing 29; case study regarding 54–5; faculty perceptions of 22–4; nonverbal 27–8; as problematic for ASD students 24–5; and theory of mind 25–7; written vs. oral 12, 31–2
Council for Exceptional Children (CEC) 62
Cure Autism Now Foundation (CAN) 62

depression 14, 16, 87–8
Developmental Disabilities Assistance and Bill of Rights Act (2000) 5
Division on Autism and Development Disabilities (DADD) 62–3
DO-IT (Disabilities, Opportunities, Interworking, and Technology) 72–4
dysgraphia 18
dyslexia 14

educational accommodations 16–19, 35, 104t
Education for All Act (1975) 2
employment rate 5
executive function and dysfunction: and ASD students 11–12, 29–31; case study regarding 56–8; and central coherence ("big picture" analysis) 32–4; and contextual adaptability 31–2; definition of 29–30; faculty perceptions of 23–4; and instructional pace 32

FAME (Faculty and Administrator Modules in Higher Education) 74, 79
FAPE (free and appropriate education) 2
fluorescent lighting 13

Grandin, Temple 66–7

handwriting 18
Higher Education Act (2008) 6, 35

IDEA (Individuals with Disabilities Education Act) 2
inclusion movement 2
information processing 12–13. *See also* communication
instructional pace 32

joint attention 25–7

Kogan, M. D. 4

language. *See* communication; information processing
lecture-style classes 10, 12
legislation: Americans with Disabilities Act (1990) 5–6; Developmental Disabilities Assistance and Bill of Rights Act (2000) 5; Education for All Act (1975) 2; Higher Education Act (2008) 6, 35; IDEA (Individuals with Disabilities Education Act) 2; New Freedom Initiative (2001) 6; President's New Freedom Commission on Mental Health (2002) 5; Rehabilitation Act (1973) 6

memory 32–3

National Center on Universal Design for Learning 74–5

New Freedom Initiative (2001) 6
nonverbal communication. *See*
    communication; symbol use
note takers 18

Office of Special Education Programs
    (OSEP) 75
Ohio State University 85
Organization for Autism Research
    (OAR) 63

planning for all learners (PAL) 80
postsecondary education: and
    accommodations for ASD
    students 16–19; challenges of
    transition to 64–5; legislation
    regarding, for disabled students
    6, 35; skills necessary for success
    in 34–5
President's New Freedom
    Commission on Mental Health
    (2002) 5

readers and scribes 19
recognition networks 106f
Rehabilitation Act (1973) 6
resources: books and journal articles
    64–71; on comorbidity and
    autism 87–8; for faculty 84–7;
    organizations and agencies
    59–64; on self-determination
    89–97
Response to Intervention (RtI) 76

San Diego State University 84
self-determination 89–97
sensory integration: classroom
    strategies for 44; definition of 30;
    issues of, for ASD students 13,
    30–1

social interactions: faculty
    perceptions of 22–3; as
    problematic for ASD students
    8–10, 24–5; and theory of mind
    26–7
Sonoma State University 85
State of the Science Conference on
    Postsecondary Education 3
strategic networks 106f
strategies. *See* classroom strategies
students with Autism Spectrum
    Disorder (ASD): barriers to
    college attendance for 4;
    characteristics of 7–15;
    educational accommodations for
    16–19; employment rate of 5;
    faculty perceptions of 21–4,
    98–103t; and legislation
    regarding postsecondary
    education 6
symbol use 27–8

technology 19
test taking 17, 19
theory of mind 25–7
Think College 63–4

Universal Design for Learning (UDL)
    37, 71–87, 105–7. *See also*
    classroom strategies
University of Arkansas at Little Rock
    85–6
University of Connecticut Center on
    Postsecondary Education and
    Disability 86
University of Rochester 86–7
US Autism and Asperger Association
    (USAAA) 64

visual supports 37, 39–40, 65